MAURICE H. MARSH TOWNSEND

STEPPING FORWARD

My High Heel Journey of Secrets and Grit

*Stepping Forward: My High Heel Journey
of Secrets and Grit*
Copyright 2020 by Maurice H. Marsh and
Melanie Marsh Townsend

All rights reserved. No part of this publication may be reproduced or transmitted in ny form or by any means, electronic or mechanical, including photocopy, recording, or any information storage and retrieval system without express permission in writing from the publisher.

ISBN 978-1-7352249-2-3

Printed in the United States of America

ACKNOWLEDGEMENTS

To my college professor, Mrs. Glenda Maddox, for her encouragement to publish these true stories, I owe her a world of gratitude.

To my husband, daughter, sister, and friends who have helped support me during the writing and publishing of this book, I am forever grateful.

A story left untold will fade in time and its value will be lost without regard. Here is my story and the intertwined lives, lies, and secrets along that journey.

DEDICATION

THIS BOOK AND THE JOURNEY of my life is dedicated to the courageous, giving, and often funny inspiration of my sister, Helen. Thirteen years older than me, she forged the way for me and lived as an example of an independent, spirited career woman in a time when working women had few options and less opportunities. As a young woman with determination and a can-do attitude, she left our little farm community and moved three hundred miles away to Houston, Texas. She worked her way up to Department Manager at Geospace and helped build galvanometers for NASA's first landing on the moon in the late 1960s. When women typically married and stayed at home, she was a single career woman who excelled in a predominately male workforce. Her spirit of happy optimism was accentuated by a heart filled with generosity and joy.

I dedicate this book and all the lessons I learned along the way about being a determined career woman who cared about her family and others to the one who lit the path for me to follow—my sister, Helen.

FOREWORD

TO UNDERSTAND THIS STORY, you need to understand life in the deep southern state of Louisiana in the mid-1960s and 1970s.

Desegregation and integration of school was still a new concept in the South. Racial inequality was commonplace, and the lines between blacks and whites were deeply rooted. The social division regarding race created a hierarchy with white men at the top. The workforce was male dominated and women were considered subordinate in the workplace.

Interstates were being built which connected major cities and brought new life to the small towns in between. The economy was growing with the economic boom of oil and gas exploration and manufacturing. Space exploration was the new frontier and NASA was revving up to put the first man on the moon.

American troops were fully engaged in the Vietnam War and this caused a divide across the country with picketing and sit-ins protesting the U.S. involvement.

The assassination of President John Kennedy in 1963 shook the country as well as the political atmosphere.

Louisiana politics were known for entrenched corruption and ties to the Mafia.

By the 1960s, most Americans had a television in their home. For the first time, a broader audience was reached and an increase in journalism and information changed not only the political awareness, but also family entertainment. A new era was dawning in Hollywood with stars like John Wayne, Cary Grant, Dean Martin, Elizabeth Taylor, Doris Day and Rock Hudson. The Beatles sprang on the scene and dominated the music world.

Fashion was heavily influenced by Jackie Kennedy's style. Pencil skirts for women and proper business attire for men in the workplace especially in the South, were the dress code. The youth had their own new-age style of love, peace, and the tie-dye, which became the iconic sign of the times.

A new generation of free-thinking women was in the workplace and inclusion was on the horizon, but in the South, it would be slow to take root.

ONE

*"To love what you do and feel like it matters,
how could anything be more fun?"*
—Katherine Graham,
first American female Fortune 500 CEO

I headed my car north on the highway that I had so often traveled. The morning breeze gently swayed the tree branches that lined the ribbon of blacktop that ran straight for miles. Shadows from the east danced with sunbeams on the hood of my car. All of nature seemed to be singing and happy on this particular September morning—it was a stark contrast to my heavy heart on this somber day.

I checked my watch. I only had two hours to get to the small farmhouse where I grew up. It sat on the Louisiana/Arkansas state line, and then I had to drive another two hours to return to Shreveport, the city I now called home. That left little to no time for me to spend with my parents, who would most assuredly want to eat and converse before I had to leave again.

Losing someone so dear to me had left me in shock. The death of someone whom I admired and respected so much was more than my heart could handle. Although we had known for six months the cancer would win and it would take him fast, I still felt totally unprepared for this day. I witnessed the weight loss and the trips in and out of the hospital. He had given me directives on how to handle his business affairs for his wife and children. His office had been packed up and cleared out, which only magnified the emptiness of his passing. He was a company partner and I was his Executive Secretary, and most of all, he was also my friend. He had opened the door for me to the journey I would take over the next few decades. He believed and trusted in me, although I was young, inexperienced, and I had much to learn. How could cancer take my dear boss and friend? No one was more optimistic, a better fighter, or had better doctors than he did, but those things did not spare him, and he lost his valiant battle.

I already missed his cheerful voice each morning, "Hey, kid, we have lots to do today so I can play golf on Wednesday afternoon and you can do your schoolwork." How lucky I was to have a boss who encouraged my growth and made it possible for me to work and continue my education. No one ever questioned my Wednesday afternoons with schoolbooks spread on my desk—my homework in progress. I guess it wasn't fair, but I was determined to attend classes at noon or sometimes at night. Six hours of college classes was an added load for me with a job, a husband, a young daughter, and home and church work. It might take several years, but I knew having my college degree would pay off.

It's surprising how fast seven years passed with my full schedule that kept me moving at such a speedy pace. I'd had a few jobs before this one, but this job with an oil and gas company was special to me. It gave me a feeling of purpose and boosted my confidence with all that I was taking part in and learning. I was in the middle of all the excitement of the corporate world, which included typing each word of every major agreement, calculating costs of drilling oil and gas wells, statistics, and prospectuses for multi-million-dollar deals. It gave me a sense of pride to be responsible for so many details and to know the company was dependent on me. All the respect and the magnitude of trust my boss, Mr. Roth, instilled in me, made my heart excited to come to work and to be a part of this group of people. After seven years with the company, I could handle the work blindfolded.

I am quite sure most jobs weren't as fun as mine and it was out of the ordinary to have the close friendship we did. As I drove along, the memories flashed through my mind of those happy days. The day I was hired, the day my boss sang in *my* Christmas choir program, the golf tournaments at the country club, the days of office fun: singing duets before we started the workday, and the day he told the big boss "dat story."

As I drove, the shadows lengthened, and the beautiful sunshine turned to dark clouds. Suddenly, I drove into a heavy downpour. Even at full speed, the wipers provided barely enough visibility as I made my way through the familiar small towns. My mother had always told me, "It rains when a good person dies." Her words echoed through my thoughts as the raindrops pounded the windshield.

I had raced through two small towns without even noticing I had passed them—not sure if I had been speeding. Luckily, I was on schedule and today that was very important. With only 30 more miles to go, I should be there on time.

Four days ago, I accepted a new job downtown. I had never imagined working for an attorney who had also been a U.S. Senator. The thought was exciting! I knew there would be a lot to learn and new challenges. He hired me on the spot and asked me to begin work on the first day of the month. It was my fallback plan. I had planned to turn the job down if my boss had beaten his battle with cancer. Mr. Roth knew that I had answered the ad in the newspaper. I told him it was just to see what was available should he decide to take a medical leave or early retirement. He asked, "Why not work for my replacement?"

My answer brought a big smile to his face when I told him, "He can't sing." I also told him, "and I hate how he is arranging our office furniture, he ordered me to make new labels…and you know he has a really foul mouth. I have to edit all my dictation notes to eliminate the GD's, SOB's and the F-ing-SOBs. His loud phone conversations full of expletives go on all day. He never plays golf on Wednesdays; please don't ask me to work for him! I will always be your secretary."

He was very pale and looked serious, then shrugged with a smile. I went to his house every day, carrying the heavy briefcase with all the folders of documents we needed to handle that day's business. It was a task I was glad to do for him. I knew it kept his mind off his struggles and gave him a purpose to keep pushing on.

The rain has stopped now. Rain…. was a reminder of the day he hired me.

Seven years earlier, an ad in the newspaper caught my attention. I submitted a resume and much to my surprise, I was called for an interview. It was pouring that day, not the light pitter-patter kind of rain, but the kind that hits the pavement with vigor. The job I had was interesting and exciting, but unfortunately my paycheck and the benefits were pretty lousy. The interview was scheduled for 3:00 p.m. The rain was coming down hard and it did not let up. My hair, my best Jackie Kennedy-lookalike suit, and heels were drenched as I entered the door of the new offices.

The receptionist politely smiled, but she seemed a little stiff. As she asked me to be seated, I stared out the window at the rain, trying to inconspicuously blot the drips from my hair. It was a busy office; people were scurrying up and down the hall. I saw one very old man shuffling along the hall in no particular hurry to be anywhere. A loud conversation from a nearby office was laced with a string of profanity that I had not heard before. As the receptionist directed me down the hall to the third door on the left, my shoes squeaked with each step from the rainwater. I tiptoed past the other offices, trying not to draw attention to myself.

I heard loud bursts of thunder and lightning outside as the rain continued. At the third door, I entered and saw an office filled with racks of tubes with labeled maps. There was a lot of rolled up paper on the desk. (Geological maps, I later learned) The grey-haired, tall, tan gentleman gave me a quick smile. He said, "I think we are having a storm, Mrs. Marsh. Thank you for coming out on such a messy afternoon. My name is Jim Roth. This interview won't take long. Can you type? Can you take shorthand? Can you answer the phone and take instructions?"

I answered, "Yes" to all of his questions.

A brief silence filled the room as he reviewed my resume. "I notice that you are involved in your church, which pleases me. You are married and have one young daughter. What's your daughter's name?"

I smiled and said, "Melanie."

"My wife and I have a daughter and a son." As he picked up a pad and pen, he said, "I'm going to give you a little test." He dictated something simple and with my shorthand skills, it was a cinch. "Now, I need you to spell one challenging word to test your spelling ability. The word is fossiliferous."

As he looked over my shoulder, he carefully sounded out the word as I typed it on the big electric IBM typewriter in front of me. He shouted, "You got it, kid! Report for work on Monday at 8:00 o'clock."

He told me the starting salary and benefits, and I was elated as I left the building. Alden, my husband, had wonderful insurance for the three of us with his job, so that was not as important, but the salary: Y-E-S! The raise was amazing. I no longer felt the rain in my hair or the soaking wet suit and shoes as I waded back through gushes of wind and rain to my car. I felt overjoyed with this new opportunity. That rainy day turned out to be my lucky day.

I would be an executive secretary to a company partner who was Senior Geologist of the Geological Department. There were three other men in the department, so I would also be typing their letters and reports.

Soon after I began the job, Mr. Roth told me my name, Maurice, did not fit me. He said he would prefer to call me "Larcy." *What...?* He even trained his children to call me "Aunt Larcy." I had often been renamed as Marsha by neighbors and friends, but this was his unique name especially for me. For seven years, when guests were not in the office and there was no need for formality, I was called Larcy—a name that became very dear to me.

My church activities included teaching an adult Sunday School Class and directing the church choir at a small Methodist Church my family joined. Mr. Roth attended a very large Baptist Church and sang in his church choir. The shared musical interest helped cement an immediate bond. Often, we rehearsed new music together before starting the day's work. Sometimes, the other employees would gather around with their cups of coffee to listen. There was always a lot of laughter and it made for a happy start to the day.

As the Holidays were approaching, Mr. Roth offered to sing in my church choir's Christmas Cantata. It was a very formal occasion and the ladies would be wearing long brocade white satin dresses, with the men in black suits. The Christmas Cantata was entitled *A Song Unending* by John Peterson.

The night of the performance was remarkable. As the choir filed into place on the risers, the organist played heavenly music for the introit. I followed in last and the pianist took her seat. I turned to the microphone to give the welcome and introduction, and was surprised by the unusually large crowd, which caused my knees to tremble. I looked out beyond the dim lights and saw about ten rows of company employees seated in the pews. Most likely, many of them had not been inside a church for a long time. The cigar-smoking rascal, the geologist named Bob, could only stand it a few minutes before, in a not-so-quiet whisper, said, "Hi, kid," which was followed by laughter from the whole audience.

After the program, I discovered some of the crowd of 300 were members of the Baptist Choir and friends of Mr. Roth. I knew then who had made this night so special and filled the church to standing room only. His support meant so much.

The music and voices filled with confidence and a smooth richness that could have only been orchestrated by the Holy Spirit. It was as if God took over and was moving my mouth and body to give the welcome and introduction through the whole performance. I felt like a vapor in the air. Alden said I had not appeared nervous and that I seemed to glow with excitement. Six years of being a choir director had led me to this wonderful moment and it now had a new deeper meaning. The group photo taken by the photographer after the performance captured the moment in time, as well as in my heart, as a lasting record.

There are so many wonderful memories of my time with Mr. Roth and the many imprints he left in my life. He will be missed but not forgotten.

As my car came down the hill and I turned in the driveway of my childhood home, it was lunchtime, and I saw that Daddy's truck was gone, but there was my sweet and precious five-foot-two mother coming out to greet me.

"Hi, Mother, where's Daddy?"

"I sent him the store to get some tea. He will be back in a minute." Her arms were around me as she said, "I'm so sorry about Mr. Roth, baby. I know he was a good man."

We walked hurriedly up the steps to the porch and passed my favorite porch swing. The familiar aromas of savory foods from the kitchen and that clean feeling of home seemed to soothe my shattered nerves. That warm hug and kind voice was comforting, and I hated to pass my room without stopping, but I rushed to mother's bedroom closet. She handed me a dress and said, "Baby, please get you a nice black dress for occasions like this. I wish I had a better one than this."

"Oh, Mother, I would so seldom wear a black dress. As long as you and I stay the same size, I'll just wear yours. Your tan and black dress is so elegant. I'll put it on in a second."

"I have some food for you; just eat it while you drive back. Daddy is going to miss seeing you. He probably met someone he knew and got delayed. You better hurry, you only have an hour and a half to make it to the funeral."

I glanced in the mirror as I pulled the pocket in place. This knit dress was perfect for me. Black paisley with a beige background, the hemline slightly above the knee, buttoned down the front, form fitting, it hugged my waist and hips. It was beautiful! Mother was back with a covered plate and a Coke. I gave her three kisses and ran for the car. I started the engine and pulled out of the driveway as I waved goodbye.

I was back on the road again, making the journey from the countryside where I grew up to the city I now called home. The air felt crisp with opportunities of my new future, but my mind was fragmented with memories of the past. As I glanced in the mirror, I noticed my eyes looked swollen from tears. I tried to remember the good times.

The older gentleman, Mr. Abramov, who shuffled up and down the hall looking into the offices, was a senior partner and founder of the company. He was a Russian-born Jew. His office was straight across the hall from mine and I often heard him curse out employees when they drilled a dry well. His typical rants were mostly ignored except for these times. But I knew him to be a kind man.

Mr. Abramov told me his wife had died just two months before I started to work there. The company grapevine alleged that his wife's half of the fortune was $80,000,000 and was to be divided between their two children. Money did not seem that important to him, although he was proud about what he had accomplished in his life.

Mr. Abramov had told me that he started earning his own living at age six, selling bananas in New York City. Although he had been a hard worker from a very young age, it was a known fact that he could not read or write. Often, he would bring a magazine or newspaper that had a picture of something for sale and ask me. "What does *dat* say?" I was happy to interpret for him.

I know he did not ask me about one particular ad. Several years after his wife passed away, a mail-order girlfriend arrived from New York. She took a cab from the airport straight to our building. Mr. Abramov brought her into my office, but in a moment of nervousness, could not think of my name. She had bright red hair, fancy clothes, and a fur coat and was wearing bright bold lipstick and tall stiletto heels. She was a dramatic contrast to the shuffling elderly Jewish man. It lasted about a week and he sent her back!

Mr. Roth was a deeply religious man and devoted to his faith and the Word of God. I often overheard the two men discussing their different faiths. During Christmas, Mr. Roth would share the story of Mary and Joseph and the birth of Jesus. Mr. Abramov would shake his head, unable to accept the notion of a virgin birth. Mr. Roth would end the story by pronouncing, "Jesus was the Savior of the World, he is the Messiah."

Mr. Abramov would continue to shake his head and respond emphatically, "No, no, I tell you, no, he was just a good man."

My curiosity drove me to search out and understand the Jewish faith. I knew a kind Jewish man who had worked in the pipe yard. He had worked for Mr.

Abramov seven days a week for many years, although the two seemed to have a contentious relationship. On several occasions, he would drop by my office when the bosses were out to have coffee and when I asked him, he was willing to share with me the teachings of his and Mr. Abramov's Jewish faith.

TWO

The Envelope

*"There is no time for cut-and-dried monotony.
There is time for work. And time for love.
That leaves no other time."*
—Coco Chanel

The May golf tournaments had been a delight for me. Mr. Roth was Secretary/Treasurer for the tournament, which put him right in the middle of the event. It was the Annual Oilmen's Golf Tournament and was a week full of fun. It was my job to send out the invitations to oil companies in Arkansas, Louisiana, Mississippi, and Texas and ask for contributions and fees.

I collected the funds and kept meticulous records each year. Those companies that did not give generously were looked down upon and considered "weak" thereafter. Sets of golf clubs, luggage, and other gifts and prizes were purchased to be given away. First prize was

$100,000— cash! Second prize was $25,000 and third prize was $10,000—that was some serious cash.

I got to keep the money at home, under the bed (my husband's idea of a safe place) until the day of the tournament.

The tournament was the largest ever held for the oil and gas men in the Ark-La-Tex area. Mr. Roth and his committee spent a lot of time pairing the teams and planning the activities for the ladies such as bridge games, food, and live bands. It was a first-class tournament all the way! The winner's table was set up in the clubhouse and I had the cash winnings in $100 bills bundled ready to hand out. $100,000 stacked for the first-place winner, $25,000 for the second-place winner, and $10,000 for third place. I had never seen a stack of loot like that and holding on to it was a powerful feeling.

The last play of the day pushed into the evening just before sunset. The top place would go to a newcomer from Arkansas. It was a long but fun day and though I recognized many other ladies who attended, I knew none of them by name. My mother would be crushed to know I did not eat the delicious food they had prepared. I only drank a Coke to get me through the day. When it was over, I celebrated the conclusion of the events and was welcomed in the arms of my sweet husband as he said, "Sugg, I'm taking you out to eat."

At 8 o'clock in the morning, the message came for me to rush to the hospital. Mr. Roth's son said, "Dad is back in the hospital this morning Aunt Larcy, and he said for you to come soon."

I grabbed my briefcase with a shorthand pad and pen and raced to the hospital. My heart was racing, and I barely remember the drive there. As I stepped off the elevator, searching for his room, I was met in the hallway by Mr. Roth's son and daughter. They both looked anxious and asked me to please hurry to his room. The door opened and I raced to his bed. He reached for my hand and I clasped it tightly. My heart was heavy as I looked into his face and saw how pale and weak he was. It was the look of his looming death and there was nothing I could do but be there for him. He asked his children to leave the room for just a few minutes.

As they walked out of the room, he smiled at me with the twinkle in his eyes growing dim, and he said, "Kid, the time has come for you to handle all the things that I need you to do and have prepared you for. Do you remember the secret envelope that no one is to read?"

"Yes, I do, Mr. Roth."

He turned his head towards me and said, "It's time to put the stamp on it and get it in the mail—this morning please. Never let my family know about the envelope, OK?"

I promised him once again, just as I had so many years ago.

He continued, "Then tomorrow, you need to convert the accounts and instruct my little lady how to take over the bank accounts and bills. She has only had her personal account to manage until now. You are *it*, kid—you have to handle all the details and make the transition."

"Oh, no," I said, "This won't need to be done now, you are going to get better."

He smiled sweetly with a calm resolve despite the waxy look on his sweaty face. "Thank you for everything, Larcy, every day was a super great one. Good luck in the new job; I hope it's a good one. Now, go and hurry to the post office for me." He turned his head to the window and gazed out as I left the room.

The calm resolve made the finality of his request heavy on my heart. I hurried past the family in the hall and told them to call if they needed anything. Rushing back to the office, I wondered again about the letter I was about to mail.

I thought back to the early days when Mr. Roth first told me about the secret envelope and his very specific instructions. The thought of him actually asking me to mail it was now met with the reality of his death. I had never questioned the contents of the large brown envelope or why it was such a secret. I respected whatever his reasons were and knew it must be very important to him. He entrusted me with something so important that even his wife was not aware of the secret envelope. When I was given instructions years ago, I jokingly told him, "This mystery letter must be about a murder or a mysterious crime." He laughed *just a little* and said it concerned something that happened 20 years ago.

Why didn't he mention this to his family? I didn't think to ask at the time, but I wish I had. I guess the letter was important to Mr. Roth and Mr. Hadley in Mississippi, to whom it was addressed. I had never heard him mention his name in reference to any business matter. If it was something that happened 20 years ago, it would have been in the late 1940s or early '50s. What could have been so important that he carried the secret to his death? And what difference would it make to Mr. Hadley so many years later? As I dropped the sealed letter in the mailbox at the post office, all I had were unanswered questions. I would never understand Mr. Roth's last request but continued to contemplate it for many years. I guess not all questions get answered.

"Some secrets are meant to be kept forever."
—Liane Moriarty

When I returned to the office, there was a message waiting for me that Mr. Roth had passed away 30 minutes after I left him. My heart was filled with sadness, but I was pleased that I could fulfill his last request and I was glad he could trust me to carry out his last wish.

The family planned the funeral for 2:00 p.m. the following day, which seemed really quick, but this was their decision and maybe there were reasons I did not know.

The next day, to my shock, the funeral was held in the cemetery, not a church or funeral home. For a man who was so involved in his church, this seemed an odd choice. Knowing how much his church meant to him and how large his church community was, this did not make sense to me. This was like no funeral I had seen before. Hundreds of people were in the cemetery gathered around the burial site. Of course, with only a few rows of folding chairs for family, people were standing as close as possible in hopes to be able to hear the minister. Mr. Roth's son ran to greet me, "Hurry, Aunt Larcy, Momma has been looking everywhere for you."

"Why? We still have 15 minutes."

"She wants you to walk in the procession beside her."

It was, for sure, an honor and I did feel like family, but the feeling was masked with a bit of anger. So many times over the years, Mrs. Roth had been removed and uncaring. Her weekly bridge games always seemed to be a higher priority than her concern for her husband. She was a stark contrast to his happy outgoing personality. Usually disconnected from feelings of compassion for others or involvement in much more than her own pleasures, I was hoping she didn't ruffle my feathers anymore with her hasty sharpness.

Mrs. Roth saw me approach and said, "Where on earth have you been? We have been calling everywhere for you."

I responded with a controlled, "Sorry, I am here now." Tears were pouring out of my eyes and my heart felt as if there was a hole in it. Losing someone like Mr. Roth who had been my mentor and friend was painful. As the eulogy was about to begin and in my midst of pain, I noticed not one of his family members were crying. They all seemed to be joking and laughing as they made their way to their seats near the casket. This was not the reaction I expected at such a somber occasion. I heard very little of what the minister said as my mind was trying to make sense of this. A large church choir began to sing, but their voices all faded into the background of my mind. As the Amen was spoken, Mrs. Roth leaned towards me and whispered, "I'll be at the office in the morning to meet with you."

"Ok," I replied.

She seemed very detached from what we had just been a part of, putting to rest such a good and honorable man. *How could her mind be wandering to business matters as she was laying her husband to rest? Where was her feeling of loss and sadness?* I wondered.

As the service ended and I walked past his beautiful casket, no one could hear my trembling soft words, "Dear Mr. Jim Roth, your life is worthy of remembering and retelling. You were educated, successful, talented and kind. You were a man of character and class! Thank you for being my friend. I hope you sing with the angels some of the songs we sang together."

THREE

"The man who can keep a secret may be wise, but he is not half as wise as the man with no secrets to keep."
—Edgar Watson Howe

As I sat at the vanity applying my makeup, I sipped my morning coffee and contemplated the start of my new job. There was a rush of new expectation in my life. New opportunities and new possibilities were ahead of me.

The usual 8:00 a.m. rush hour would change to an easier 9:00 a.m. arrival time. This would be a real bonus. It gave me leisure time to take little Melanie to school rather than hurry and rush her out of the car as I had to do so often. So many times, I felt as if I had abandoned her for the 30-minute wait before the school bell rang. It had been very common for me to get to work late because I was caught by the train crossing two blocks from the office. It was usually a tight morning schedule.

I could now look forward to leaving work at 4:30 rather than 5:00 p.m. It was news to me that attorneys had short work hours, but it was great news!

My paycheck would be much better, and I would be paid every two weeks.

The new office was located right in the heart of downtown and my dress code would need to be somewhat upgraded. Suits, heels, and hose were going to be my new standard. Another sip of coffee and a quick hair spray helped me prepare for my day. I remembered at the interview seeing others in fluffy scarves, see-through blouses with pretty petticoats and camisoles showing through. Their shoes had bare heels or bare toes or both. This was a new and exciting place of fashion and style.

Shopping would be really convenient and fun! It was just a short walk across the street from the office to my favorite stores. New and different eating places were sprinkled everywhere—even inside stores and church basements, as well as on the corners. There was a large cafeteria on the third floor of a nearby office building. Everything was within walking distance of the office. The hustle and bustle of downtown seemed to send an electric energy of excitement through the air.

Melanie and I were in the car on our way to her school. She felt my excitement and we sang little songs together as we made our way through the stop lights. School buses were ahead of us bumping along as we wove in and out of the traffic. I thought to myself, *Never will my sweet little girl ride with those sweaty, mean kids packed on a bus!* I adored our morning rides as we started our day together.

As we pulled up to the school, there were children jumping rope and running around the playground, and teachers watching the children. Now we could use every minute of that time to sit together in the car until the bell rang. As I began to brush Melanie's long blonde hair, I thought, *How wonderful this time together is, not having to rush and being able to take a second look at her homework and count her coins for lunch.*

She asked me, "Mom, what do you do at work?"

I smiled and said, "I am a secretary—another word for secret keeper."

She looked at me with a confused smile, "You keep secrets for work?"

"Sometimes I do," I replied. She put her little arms around my neck, gave me a hug and kiss, and I watched her skip all the way to her classroom.

I drove away humming and singing with a happy feeling in my soul as I made my way towards downtown. It was six miles from the school to downtown and traffic was not bad at this time of morning. My mind kept going back to the final day last week; getting Mr. Roth's business moved to his home had been fairly simple. I was surprised that Mrs. Roth could convert a room into an office so quickly, but she did. The dark wood desk was so beautiful in the room she had set up.

She had hired a CPA to greet me at the new home office. Mr. Hal Simpson would handle her millions in the bank and her investments. I handed him the insurance policies that totaled $1,000,000. I had paid those premiums quarterly for seven years without really thinking of the time they would be disbursed to his wife. She did not have time or want to discuss any details; she was late for bridge. The many boxes of files I packed and labeled with a few notes inserted for clarification were scattered here and there. "Just cover it with Hal," she said. "Good luck, Hal," as she left for her all-important bridge game. I guess this transition in her life would not be one she cared to understand or deal with. Hal and I covered the details he would need to know to handle what was left behind. As our time ended and I turned the page on that chapter in my life, I could only be grateful for having been his Larcy.

I stopped humming and singing as I entered Main Street and looked for the parking garage. It would be really nice to have valet parking. I arrived relaxed and calm 15 minutes early to my new office. A co-worker, Diane, was there to greet me. "The boss will be late every day," she said.

I could use this extra time to ride the elevator back down to the ground floor and pick up a cup of coffee. Buying coffee every day was not to my liking, especially because I had to carry a tiny Styrofoam cup filled with hot coffee back up the elevator. Just as I settled into my chair, Mr. Crenshaw, my boss, came into the office. ***Perfect timing,*** I thought. He was beaming and happy to see me. He quickly reviewed with Diane the "did-you-dos." He sat down on top of my desk and explained that "Di-yan" (as he called her) would handle the load of typing and filing. I was his Executive Secretary, so I would handle clients and his appointments and keep him on track with his workload. He discovered my Styrofoam cup of coffee, picked it up and started sipping it. "You, my dear, will do the notary work, close loans, and I think you will find fun in keeping up." He finished the last drop of my coffee, took off his hat, and strolled to his adjoining office.

Diane giggled softly and said, "It's going to definitely be fun!" She stacked a tall stack of files on my desk for me to proofread before passing them on to Mr. Crenshaw. It felt like a perfect way to start, reviewing court cases on divorces, wills, and bodily injury cases. There was even a Fannie Mae Home Loan to review. It had six carbon copies for each page (this is before the days of auto-correct).

Our first client of the day was a lightly colored young African American man. He had little to say to me except, "Tell the boss Larry is here. Sometimes he makes me wait, sometimes he don't."

I entered Mr. Crenshaw's office to announce his visitor, Larry. He asked me to first come in and I shut the door. Once the door was completely closed, he said, "Larry will come once a week, so I guess I should tell you the story." He looked out the window, pointed and said, "Do you see the white building in the factory complex over yonder?" There was a magnificent view of the city from his ninth-floor window. He cleared his throat and said, "The owner of that factory had a bit of a problem. He is an important upstanding man and has been a client of mine for about 15 years.

"Years ago, he had an inappropriate relationship with a woman. Larry is his illegitimate son. He needs to keep that quiet so that it doesn't damage his reputation. I handle the funds in cash for him to support Larry. I dole out the money to him weekly. His mother used to come by, but now he usually comes alone, always asking for more money than is allotted. Send him in and greet our next client while I get Larry out of our hair." There was a somber silence as I walked out of the office as he continued to stare out the large windows that overlooked the factory.

By the time I returned to my office, there were three clients waiting patiently around the room. It was a group of men forming a new construction business who needed Mr. Crenshaw to prepare an agreement for them to form their corporation. For me, this meant dictation and a new world of terminology in shorthand. The changes of the new job made the day go quickly. Diane helped me get Mr. Crenshaw ready for his 2:00 court date. We ate sandwiches at our desk and worked straight through lunch, typewriters clicking fast as papers stacked up on our desks.

When the boss returned from lunch, he asked me to track down where he had left his hat. He had made four stops during lunch and had no clue where he left it.

Great, now I am doing detective work, I thought. I began calling until I finally found the lost chapeau. He sent "Di-yan," as he called her, to get the hat and meet him at the courthouse.

Diane was five years younger than I and was married with a son. Her son was named Charles II but she often called him "two." She had told me that Mr. Crenshaw and his wife had six children, five girls and one boy. We tried to keep this in mind on those days he came in a bit cranky or absentminded.

Every day was filled with new and exciting cases and things to learn. I was grateful to have a boss who was kind and willing to teach me the legal world of which I had no knowledge. In fact, my disillusionment of the legal system was a bit amusing to him. He often chuckled at my outspoken opinions and sense of right and wrong.

The first time I saw the boss meet with a divorce attorney, they propped their feet up on the desk and dictated a brief for their court case. It blew my mind; it was the exact words they would say in court, like an orchestrated dance they would perform. After I typed it, I made three copies, one for each attorney and one for the judge. They had ironed out the "I say," and "You say," – all the details down to the pauses in between. After many laughs and cups of coffee, they had decided what the divorce settlement would be. It was agreed upon by the two men and they delivered the copy to the judge before the hearing. This seemed so unethical to me! Two men deciding the future and agreements for people over laughs and coffee. Not what I had expected in such a life-altering legal transaction.

Weeks flew by and my friendship with "Di-yan" had deepened. It felt as if we had been friends for life. We walked to the stores during lunch hours, ate together, and shared stories and problems with each other. We shared a great connection. Whenever Mr. Crenshaw was in a disgruntled mood with one of us, we stood together in giving him the icy treatment. If he treated one of us less than pleasantly, he got it from both of us! He soon caught on to this game. One day, he came to the office in a particularly bad mood. Just before he slammed the door to his office he said, "Hey, girls, I am on to your little pouting game. I have five girls at home and I have experienced it before so defrost yourselves and find the lost file!"

Files were stacked high on his desk and all had papers hanging out the sides – those were his reminders. There were stacks of files on the windowsills and along the walls on the floor. He would not let us file them in the filing cabinets because those were his "working files" and he was afraid he would forget if they were out of sight. He had walls of bookshelves filled with legal books. Mr. Crenshaw could tell me the exact book to pull for a reference or a sample contract or will. This made it easy for me to fill in the blanks.

The workload grew heavier and I grew in knowledge and confidence. I loved this job! The $100 raise that came after six months made my life wonderful. But September brought unexpected changes for me. The phone rang on my desk; it was Alden. We never talked during the day while I was working so this took me by surprise. He said, "Sugg, I have some bad news." I propped my elbows on my typewriter, pressed the receiver to my ear, and braced for the news. "Everyone was notified this morning that the glass factory (where he worked) is closing in 30 days. Those who have worked here for 30 years will be given retirement packages and some others will be placed across the country in other factories." His department would be the last to leave, but then he would be without a job after 26½ years of working there. His voice quivered as he said, "We will think through it when we get home. Try not to worry. I love ya."

All I could feel was dazed and numb. We had a beautiful new home, two cars, a new ski boat, two lake lots and monthly payments on all of them! We had shared expenses with my parents and my sister on a lake house. There was no way we could drop the ball without losing everything.

My husband was not prepared for any trade jobs and after 26 years, no other job experience to turn to. Unemployment checks would not be enough. We began to pray! September had not ended, yet I knew God would provide somehow.

A few days passed, I received another personal call at work. The call was from Mr. Crenshaw's previous personal secretary. She said, "You don't know me, but I once had your job and I would like to talk to you when it's convenient." Since the boss was away, I took her call and listened as she explained that while she had this position, she also worked a really great second job, which she had kept for the last three years. "Now I need a replacement for that job and I am offering it to you, if you are interested in a second part-time opportunity. I can go over the details with you and then introduce you to my boss this afternoon after work." This was too good to be true—just at the time I needed it the most!

I would be a secretary/bookkeeper for a very wealthy prestigious lady. The office was in her home and the hours were 5:00 p.m. to 10:00 p.m. two or three days a week. The hourly pay was even more than my present job paid. The lady was a client of my boss. Her files filled four drawers at the law firm, but there had been no activity since I had been there with any of her files.

I kept this phone call to myself as I hurried to the restroom to regroom myself for the 5:00 p.m. interview. As I drove to the affluent part of the city, I saw gardeners out working in the beautiful lawns filled with colorful flower gardens. I followed the map I had sketched from the phone instructions. These homes were sprawling two-story mansions, twisting and turning through the streets. Some even looked like castles. I was in awe! After several turns, I found the large white brick mansion of Mrs. Beatrice Galloway Winningham. The long circle drive led to the front with brick steps up to the huge double doors. I started to think about the interview and what I would say. My mind had been distracted with amazement at this magnificent home. Just then, a large black man wearing a white coat opened my car door and called me by name. He said he would show me the way to Mrs. Winningham and Brenda, who had called me about the position.

I followed close behind him as I walked through the large impressive doors; the ceilings were tall, the floors were marble with plush rugs, paintings, and fine furnishings around the room. This was a magnificent mansion and coming from a small country town, I had never seen anything like this. He led me to the meeting room, which he called the "Garden Room." Brenda and Mrs. Winningham stood to make introductions and greet me.

Brenda was a lady in her fifties who looked like a stereotypical secretary in her black horn-rimmed glasses. Mrs. Winningham was elegant and stately, like a beautiful queen. She had perfect skin and features that were shown off by the hair swept high on her head with perfect curls and styling.

We were seated at a large glass table. Her hands were beautiful and white with bright red nail polish. The ring on her finger was a huge brilliant diamond. My eyes were glued to it since I had never seen a diamond that big.

Both ladies were talking about the office duties and what I would be expected to do. Mrs. Winningham said dinner would be served at 6:00 p.m. and that she wanted me to eat with her. This was very unexpected, and I was glad my mother had trained me well in the skills of good table manners.

Emmanuel, the man in the white jacket, served Brenda and me a fruit drink with a pineapple chunk and a cherry floating on top. I noticed Mrs. Winningham's drink did not look like ours, not quite so fruity....

We strolled through the hallway back to the home office. The office was about 30' x 40' with a magnificent desk that I was told belonged to her first husband who was a doctor. One wall was a panel of fine mahogany wood doors. Brenda opened them to show me the many file drawers that lay behind them. Behind one door was a steel vault door, which looked interesting. Another door hid half-gallon bottles of hard liquor. There was a tall swivel leather chair at the desk and a fine velvet chair next to the desk. There was even a color TV across the room. What an elaborate office for a part-time gig!

Brenda pulled out some large heavy ledgers to give me a glance at the size of the bookkeeping job I would be doing. There was a weekly payroll and several bank accounts to reconcile. I could tell it was not a small task.

Brenda promised to come the next two afternoons to help me get started. I was relieved to have her help and accepted the job.

As we left the big house and walked slowly to the car, I asked Brenda why she was leaving. She smiled and said, "I have decided to spend all my evenings with my husband, wear jeans, and go barefoot, but I know it will be a grand experience for you just as it was for me for the last three years. I will see you Thursday afternoon and we will get you started."

Driving home and processing all we had discussed, darkness hindered my view except for the occasional streetlights. *Did I just dream this?* Then I heard a voice say, "This job will rescue your family," and a peace came over me. *Thank you, Lord, I knew you would provide just as you have promised.* My heart leaped with joy and a reassurance that things would be fine for my family and me. I could not wait to get home and share the good news with Alden and Melanie. I knew they would be in awe of the great new posh job that had been placed at my feet. I began to sing church songs as I drove down the freeway from darkness to streetlights that was now free from the usual traffic.

My mind started processing my new schedule. Choir practice on Wednesday nights and one night a week for my college classes would mean a full week for me. What could I give up or trade off? Bridge with my three dear friends, all entertaining, and eating out would have to be put on hold. After all, this was just a temporary job until Alden got a new one. I didn't have a clue, but this was my plan when I accepted the new job.

It was only 7:30 p.m. when I pulled into the carport at home. My sweet little Melanie came running out the door to meet me with her dad trailing behind. "Did you get it, Momma? Did you get it?"

"Yes, yes, darling, let me tell you all about it."

Alden smiled and said, "Dinner is ready for you, Sugg."

"Let's eat so I can tell you about this gorgeous big house with a long, winding staircase in the middle. The beautiful classy lady that lives there has a maid, a cook, and a chauffeur. She looked like a queen in a beautiful satin and brocade dress. Her hair was swept up on top of her head in curls. She was impressed that I was continuing my education. She has her master's degree in music. I saw a very large grand piano in a room all by itself. Oh, and the diamond ring she was wearing, you can't even imagine. It was as big as an Easter egg."

Melanie's little eyes stretched wide as I told her about the queen and her mansion—I would now be working in such a grand and special place. The chatter didn't stop until the lights went out and we were all in our beds.

FOUR

"There ae two kinds of secrets, the ones we keep from others and the ones we keep from ourselves."
—Frank Warren

Mornings brought a new surge of energy and understanding of quality time. The drive to school was more relaxed. I could listen to my little angel tell me about her friends and the teachers as we were waiting for the school bell to ring. I could brush her precious blonde hair one more time before sending her out to face her day. Some mornings we would sing together and some mornings we rode quietly, but the time together was priceless. After several mornings of sitting in the car together waiting for the bell to ring, she finally told me why she didn't want to get out of the car until *after* the first bell rang.

In her sweet little soft voice, she said, "All the kids are jumping rope before school and I don't know how."

With a new compassion for all the previous times I had been late to work and even now having to wait for the bell to ring, I said, "Oh, my darling, we can fix that," and with that reassurance, she got out of the car and skipped towards her classroom. *Guess I better plan some time in the driveway for a few lessons,* I told myself.

My drives down the interstate to the law firm were my planning sessions. Often, I pulled out a pen and paper to scribble notes with one hand while driving with the other. I had a lot going on and was juggling many tasks at the same time. This was valuable time to organize my day and even do a quick grocery list.

The work at the law firm began to get much heavier. The more I needed my morning coffee, the more I found Mr. Crenshaw sitting on top of my desk drinking the last drop. On the occasions I would try and outsmart him and bring two cups of coffee, he would not show up until noon. Diane did not drink coffee, but we usually got to have a good laugh if I got to drink my coffee before he got there or if I ended up with one extra cold cup. There was no predicting his schedule. There was usually a morning ritual of "Di-yan" getting called into his office to find lost files and papers.

As the months passed, the constant hunt for his hat turned into now finding the hat, his coat, his umbrella, and of course, the files and his briefcase. It was a daily "where's Waldo?" situation.

One day, Mr. Crenshaw called from the courthouse just ten minutes before his 2:00 p.m. case was to begin.

"Honey, I don't have my brief." He was talking about the masterpiece I had spent hours typing. Twenty pages of "I say, you say." His whole orchestrated court case was lost. (This was at a time where computers did not exist, so the only copies would be carbon pages.)

"Where do you think it is?" I muttered as I rolled my eyes at Diane. "Would you get Di-yan to look in the men's room while you hold the door open. Tell her to run as fast as she can and bring it to me. Thank you, babe."

After a heavy sigh of "Oh, God," the race was on and the brief was indeed inside the men's room on the back of the commode. Diane and I had a good laugh thinking about him sitting there practicing his script for the case.

The client overload kept our typewriters smoking. Some days were pure chaos! We would search and search for files that could not be found. Mr. Crenshaw would say, "Girls, let's stop everything and get organized. Of course, we could not help but burst out laughing since he was the most unorganized one of us all. To get us to stop laughing he would say, "Get ahold of your bearings, girls!" That only made us laugh harder and sent us running to the ladies' room out of control. We would often break out in laughter, looking across the typewriters at each other thinking of all the times he lost things that we would have to go searching for—too many times to count.

The second job was moving into a more familiar pattern, but the setting was not a relaxed one. The earlier I would slip out of the law office to get there, the happier Mrs. Winningham would be. However, everyone was always waiting for my arrival to begin dinner. There were two maids in the kitchen, but Emmanuel served Mrs. Winningham and me. After that, the kitchen could be cleaned and they could leave for the evening. Emmanuel lived in his quarters on the premises in a very small apartment off the garage.

Emmanuel told me that their daily events were preparing for my arrival and dinner to be served at the dining table three times a week. It seemed to be the highlight of her days. Mrs. Winningham was a night person. She went to bed at 2:00 or 3:00 a.m. and slept until 2:00 p.m. or, at least, stayed in bed until then. Bonnie, the beautician, came twice a week to the house. Emmanuel showed me the room with all the equipment and supplies in what looked like a grand New York salon. I placed Bonnie's weekly paycheck on the table inside the desk calendar.

The maids, Emmanuel, a yardman and a farm foreman who often had helpers were on my weekly payroll list. I paid myself twice a month, which was nice.

Mrs. Winningham would eat a light dinner. She was very proper, a little stiff, and most definitely emotionally removed. Although she answered my questions about names that appeared, I knew better than to pry into someone's personal life. She seemed to focus more on my life. We talked about me having one child, a daughter, and she told me she had a son. His father was her first husband who was a doctor who died suddenly at the age of 42. She was an only child and the daughter of an insurance executive who had done very well financially. Some of her assets included four large farms with tenants, a hospital, and her previous home, which were all a collection of the wealth of her father and her former husbands.

She had a granddaughter, Stephanie, who was Melanie's age, and suggested they meet one afternoon and play together. "I will tell Charlie (her name for Mr. Crenshaw) to let you off early." I guess now was the time to inform Mr. Crenshaw of my second job!

Each evening, Mrs. Winningham would take her place in her chair in the office next to my desk and watch me work. She would have me ring for Emmanuel on the intercom system to assist her to the bathroom door or refill the crystal glass she clutched in her hands with those beautiful red nails. Emmanuel was no spring chicken, but he would make the trips to the kitchen at the other end of the house with a slight limp in his step, faithfully serving her every need. Mrs. Winningham was able to walk, but with the years of drinking taking its toll on her body, her movement was slow and with caution.

That particular night, he assisted her to the bathroom door, and walked back to the office doorway and said, "I heard her say she planned to have Miss Stephanie over to play with Miss Melanie. Well, don't hold your breath, she ain't coming. She don't speak with her son; he hates her. She thinks you will call them and get Miss Stephanie over here, but they will just hang up the phone. She ain't told you about her son, Everett? She's coming back, I'll tell you about him later, but he ain't no good!"

We could see Mrs. Winningham coming slowly down the hall. Emmanuel whispered, "It won't be long until she has to go back to the hospital." She had never discussed her health issues with me, but I could tell he was very familiar with her repeating cycles of overindulging and attempts at detoxing.

She finally settled back in her tall velvet chair beside my desk. I had finished writing the checks to six country clubs for membership dues. I mentioned that my former boss and his wife had been a member of a couple of the country clubs and asked if she knew them. "Oh no, I never attend any of those places. Give me a good reason why I should." I was astounded and said with encouragement, "They have wonderful food, live entertainment, and dances."

With her head held high and her body posture ever so straight, she said, "My dear, I can have anything I want served under glass at my table. I can hire the chefs and all their helpers if I like. That is how I got Emmanuel. I hired him away from H.L. Hunt. Did he tell you? I just gave him more money than H.L. and he now belongs to me."

"Oh no, Emmanuel did not tell me he had worked for Mr. Hunt."

"Yes, my dear, money will buy you anything if you have enough of it. I used to enjoy cruises, but I don't take cruises anymore because I don't like being with a lot of people that act like fools. I have been everywhere and done it all. Let me tell you about my second husband, Mr. Brunswick." Her hands trembled as she took another sip of her cocktail from a crystal glass. Then she pressed the newly installed buzzer on top of my desk to ring for Emmanuel. I figured she needed a refill to finish her story.

With a fresh drink in hand, she continued, "Mr. Brunswick was appointed as the Ambassador to France by President Kennedy and we traveled everywhere together. I have trophies and awards for golf tournaments that I participated in on every amazing golf course in and out of this country. We stayed at the finest hotels with all the amenities. For six glorious years, my clothes were packed in and out of luggage as we traveled the world together. We saw every mountain and seashore; we saw every old rock that anyone had named. My friend Charlie encourages me to take trips now, but it isn't any fun alone. If you, or you and Melanie could go with me, I would take you anywhere in the world you would like to go."

I turned in my chair to look at her face. She was very serious and very sincere. "What a wonderful treat that would be. I hope we can do that."

She looked over her glass and said, "Can you go?"

"Well, I need to get my husband back to work, and my mother is not doing well. She is undergoing some tests, but I will give it some thought. It would be so exciting." I could read the disappointment in her face. I knew with all my responsibilities that it would be next to impossible, but it was such a wonderful offer.

The checks were arranged in stacks and deposit slips made out for the banks. "You have a lot of dividend checks, Mrs. Winningham. "Yes, I owe that to my third husband."

Third? Things were getting interesting. I stopped writing and started placing stamps on the envelopes. "Did something happen to Mr. Brunswick?"

"Yes, my one true love was killed in a plane crash in Australia. It was devastating, and my life was ruined. I moved back to Shreveport and bought this house. I am an only child and both my parents are gone. My mother died before I was married to Mr. Brunswick. My father was cared for by caretakers and I called daily until his extended hospital stay was over. I'm sorry to say, we had a bad disagreement before he passed away five years ago.

"Now, my third husband was a stockbroker. Rueben invested lots of my money in the stock market. He lived and breathed the *Wall Street Journal* and every company report and financial statement he could read. I don't do anything with the stocks now, other than take the dividend checks to the bank, keep up with the splits, and clip the coupons for the bank deposits. That's now a part of your job. I'll call Charlie and tell him I need you one afternoon to go with me to the bank.

"We need to get to the safe deposit box and go through the papers, so you can clip the coupons."

"I have never clipped those kind of coupons, Mrs. Winningham."

"I'll show you how. I have several bonds for cities and states. They pay interest to me by clipping coupons that are attached maturity dates. Some are semi-annual or annual or whenever I get to the box and clip them."

She called my boss to ask for the extra time to go to the bank. As he sat on my desk sipping *my* coffee as he usually did, he said, "Mrs. Winningham called to ask permission to use you tomorrow at 1:00. She says you are helping her with her books at night. I think that is good. Maybe you can help her get off the hooch. So far, no one else has been successful. She won't listen to her doctors; she won't take heed to what I say either. I have known her for many, many years. I handled all four of her husband's successions, so I feel compelled to continue helping her."

"Did you say *four?*"

With a nod of his head and a grin, he said, "Yes, I sure did. Right there in our files behind you are all the details of her four marriages."

Surprised by the news, I replied, "She told me about three. I didn't hear the last name of the stockbroker husband, I had just assumed it was Winningham."

He smiled big and looked me in the eye and said, "Not so, babe."

"Are you sure it is ok to leave at 1:00? Diane might not show up again tomorrow. She might be still battling morning sickness."

"That's true, but I will just stick a note on the door and lock it. Maybe I will take a little nap and then roll up my sleeves and get some work done. Go ahead and help the poor soul."

Driving through the stately neighborhood, with all the manicured landscaped yards in the daylight seemed a bit unfamiliar from my late evening routine. The mansion was illuminated in the noon sunshine and the rose garden was in full bloom with vibrant colors. My car had barely stopped before Emmanuel opened my door. He directed me to the long white limousine parked outside the garage. He looked sharp dressed in his chauffeur's uniform, a white pressed shirt, black tie, shiny shoes, and a black chauffeur's hat. He told me to wait at the limo until he got the boss. The change in her since I had seen her two days ago was drastic. She entered, sliding each foot while holding tightly to Emmanuel. As she stepped into the limo, I got a glance at her swollen feet and ankles. It was a bit shocking and looked painful. Her beautiful expensive shoes were stretched to the limit. The hairdresser, Bonnie, had dressed her in a designer black pantsuit.

Emmanuel motioned for me to be seated beside Mrs. Winningham and said he would return soon and closed the car door.

Limos are for funerals, I thought. Guess I had seen them in the movies with a mobster and his chauffeur or with movie stars getting out of them on a red carpet, but I never imagined I would be riding in one going to the bank. My eyes scanned the car looking at all the amenities, the small TV, a full bar with expensive decanters, crystal glasses, and an ice compartment. This was nicer than some kitchens I had been in.

Emmanuel returned. He placed an ice bucket full of ice in the wet bar. He prepared a glass of lemonade for me and passed a highball crystal glass of the hooch to the *Queen.* Her shaking white hands with the beautiful long, red nails reached for the glass and hurried it to her lips for a gulp to steady her tremor.

"Getting up this early in the day has thrown me for a loop," she said.

I thought to myself, *No, Mrs. Winningham, that is not the cause; it's those highball glasses you keep in your hands.*

She held her head straight with perfect posture like Queen Elizabeth on a tour of the village. The limo parked at the side door of the bank, not the front door where everyone else comes in. The Branch Manager was expecting us. We were directed to a private office and two large bank boxes were sitting on the highly polished table in front of us. Without speaking a word, Mrs.

Winningham pointed, gave a nod with her head to turn both boxes toward me and then open them.

I opened each of the many envelopes containing municipal bonds and spread them across the table. There were too many to count. Then I searched for the maturity dates in order to clip the coupons to deposit at the bank. A flashy jewelry collection was in one drawer. Each piece was carefully shown to me with the history of each item. Yes, there were four stunning and large wedding rings belonging to her from her four husbands.

I looked at her and said, "Four?" She was unaware I had previously discussed her husbands with my boss, her attorney.

There was a bit of a hesitation as she leaned forward in her chair and blurted out, "Yes. I didn't tell you about the fourth because he was a goddamn bastard! He's dead now and that is where he deserves to be."

I was taken back by her words and could do nothing but stare into the box of jewelry. They were placed in blue velvet boxes, probably purchased for their safekeeping in this storage box. But my thoughts kept going to the fourth man. *What happened? And why did she feel so angry at the thought of him?*

I turned my head towards her, and asked, "Did you say he was dead?"

There were only the two of us in the room, but she lowered her voice and said, "Elliott Winningham was the most handsome man I have ever seen. We were married in New York. All my Washington friends came. The wedding was in grand style. But after the wedding, we went away on a month-long honeymoon. It was then he revealed his secret to me, that he preferred men to women—in bed. He said that after careful consideration and seeing the many ways we could benefit each other, he believed we could make the marriage work; therefore, he proposed to me and chose to believe I would understand. I gave him every curse word I have ever heard and caught the next plane home. When I got back, I made up excuses, hid my embarrassment, and stayed in hiding. I did discuss the matter with my friend Charlie but no one else!

Two months later, Elliott showed up at my front door with his companion, Milton. The man was polished and fine looking. They asked that I allow them to talk with me to resolve our matters. I knew that my life would not fit with this relationship between the two of them. This was not the marriage I signed up for! After discussing the social implications and embarrassment that I would endure to disguise the situation, our arrangement was that I would allow them to stay one week per month in my home during which I drank all the Old Charter in the house. To those who knew me, I said that my husband was a busy New York executive and traveled often. This worked for a brief time, until he began flaunting my generosity and acceptance.

He flew in numerous friends of his from New York for a party here in Shreveport. He hired musicians, wait staff, the whole nine yards, and partied until dawn. At the party, with his arm extended and a drink in his hand raised for a toast as a last hurrah, his body slumped over—dead—across the grand piano. It was a massive heart attack. His male companion had him cremated and then returned to New York."

There was a deafening silence. I was stunned, and I could not think of a single word to say. I looked at her wide-eyed, trying to process the story she had just told me.

Flashing the big rock on her hand, she said, "So I bought *this* diamond ring to make me feel better."

My eyes were wide with disbelief. I said, "You should write a book about your life."

With a slight smirk, she said, "I've been told that by Charlie, but my hands shake now, and I only have you a limited amount of time. That might be possible if I could have you here every day. I guess I would need to double your paycheck and take you away from Charlie. He would probably throw me out as a client. I have to walk a tightrope with keeping you both. He takes care of all sorts of legal affairs for me."

It was 4:00 p.m. The time had gone so quickly in the bank. She asked me to bring in Emmanuel to help her get out of her chair and back to the limo.

The ride back was in awkward silence. No conversation at all, just thoughts flickering through my mind of what she had told me about Mr. Winningham, his big deception, and his demise. She had a fresh glass of her hooch to keep her occupied as she looked out the window deep in thought. There was only the sound of the jingling ice in her glass as she sipped the stiff drink.

As we walked back into the mansion, all I could think was that all this wealth and extravagant luxury was a façade for the emptiness she felt. Rooms and rooms of perfectly placed things by the interior designer. A life-size painting of her hung in the formal living room. It covered most of the wall and probably took a whole year for the artist to complete. It was a beautiful portrait that reflected what she wanted the world to see, but I now saw the sadness behind the elegant grande dame.

I freshened up my hair and slowly washed my hands in the office bathroom before they called me to take my place at the table for dinner.

All the glitz and mystery of her stately persona and brilliant intelligence were diminishing before my eyes. It seemed to register differently today. How truly empty these walls really were and how helpless was this once powerful lady who now suffered from chronic alcoholism and loneliness. The crutches that were her diversions of the journeys she had traveled were now the poisons of her decline.

After dinner, we sat at the desk paying bills and totaling thousands of dollars in deposits to be made. Her speech became slurred after several of her special cocktails. Emmanuel came in to put her to bed. This seemed to be nothing out of the ordinary for him. I am sure it was part of his routine. As his 300-pound body lumbered back to her room, he returned to her chair in my office and he began talking about his exhausting night last night. In her anticipation of going to the bank, she stayed awake all night. She summoned him to cook turnip greens and cornbread for her at 1:00 a.m. She ate very little after his efforts and he got no rest. I could see the exhaustion in his eyes.

She had many recurring events and birthdays on her monthly calendar. I am not sure how many she actually knew, but each week she would select cards from a large box of Hallmark cards for me to address and mail. Tonight, it looked like I would be making those selections myself.

At the law firm the next morning, a phone call came from Emmanuel. He had rushed Mrs. Winningham to the hospital by ambulance that previous evening. She had asked him to call me to come to the hospital. I asked if I should notify her son. Emmanuel said, "He ain't goin' to come even if she's dyin'." This was a big mystery to me, something I just could not wrap my head around. *He's her only child, why would he care so little what happened to her?* I wondered.

I went to the hospital at noon and found her with her personal entourage. She was in a hospital suite with Emmanuel, who had brought her best pillows with fine satin pillowcases and her china, crystal, and silver with linen dinner napkins from home. Emmanuel was serving her on a tray and the maid, Cora, was spoon feeding her. Her legs were extremely swollen; they were black and purple. It must have been painful.

As I stood there trying not to show my shock, I said nothing, just waiting for my instructions. She wanted me to speak with her physicians. I was not sure why she wanted me to be the one, but, then again, as I was coming to understand, there was no one else beyond the people she employed. Her doctor was called to the room to speak to me about her condition. He asked me to step into the hall to speak privately. He told me they would do all they could to get the fluid out of her body as quickly as possible, but at some point, there would be nothing they could do. His tone changed as he said, "We grow angry and frustrated when she doesn't cooperate with us after we get her dried out. She immediately starts drinking alcohol when she goes home, and we have to start the process over again. We have not seen any of her family so maybe you can pass the information on to them or anyone who can help her. She specified you to receive reports about her condition. Will you be here tomorrow?"

"I'll be here again tomorrow at noon and back at 5:00 p.m. until 10:00 p.m.—as long as she is here. Do you think she will be here many days?"

With a look of serious concern, he replied, "If we are lucky again, maybe five days."

That noon hour was full of dictation and instructions. She was thinking of all the normal business to be handled. And then out of the blue, she mentioned planning a big Easter Egg hunt at her home for children.

Caught off guard, I asked, "Whose children?"

She said that her Catholic priest friend could invite the congregation, especially those with children. She asked me to call the priest and ask him to visit her in the hospital. This was the first mention of her priest or of any religious affiliation. When I called, the priest told me he barely knew her, but he would be happy to come to the hospital. With just one month away from Easter, there was not much time to prepare for such an event, but I confidently took on the task.

The second day in the hospital, she dictated instructions for the landscaping plans she wanted from the nursery. She wanted all the new plants to be in full bloom on Easter Sunday. She wanted them planted the day before, and if it took additional workers to make it happen, that was fine. She requested the design and plans to be drawn immediately for her approval. Her budget for the flowers, trimming, and mowing was $10,000 for the event. It was a bit much in my thinking, but it seemed a trivial amount in her eyes.

Next, she wanted me to contact a company to order several oversized standing rabbits for the yard, large colored eggs, and some chicks. She asked me to hire six employees from the country club for Saturday and Sunday to prepare food and dye 300 eggs. She asked me to hire a security guard and two men to valet the cars. She insisted that I bring Melanie. Her next request was the biggest of all—she wanted me to call her son and give him advance notice of the invitation to the Easter party. She wanted her granddaughter to attend this elaborate Easter party.

On the third day, when I arrived at the hospital, she was gravely ill. There was no response from her at all and the medications were not working as they had hoped. She was sleeping so deeply, it was like she was in a coma. Not wanting her to be left alone, I hired sitters to be with her around the clock. I was sure she would approve and felt better knowing she would not wake up alone.

Finally, by the fourth day, the fluid was leaving her body and there was some improvement. She was weak, but awake and asking if I had gotten all the tasks done for the party.

"Yes, I have everything on the list checked off. The nursery will have the plants by next Monday when you are home." She did not ask about the call to her son and I did not volunteer.

The truth was, I had called her son Everett who had

an unlisted number, so that took a bit of investigative skills. He was polite, a bit quiet, and listened as I identified myself and told him of his mother's condition. He said that his mother had succeeded again at getting herself in this shape and he did not offer any concern for her failing health. I moved on to tell him his mother was planning an Easter party for some children from the church and above all she wanted Stephanie there. I told him I would bring my daughter who was the same age to meet her.

He replied with sarcasm, "Oh, has she started going to church now?"

I said, "Presently, she is being treated in Willis Knighton Hospital and hopefully will be home by the weekend. Would you like me to tell her anything?" I was really appalled at his lack of concern and empathy.

"Hasn't she told you? I don't speak to my mother and Stephanie won't be attending her party. Thank you for the call." And then he hung up.

I really did not want to tell her about our conversation and thankfully, she did not ask. I wonder if she already knew. I am sure she was hoping that she would get to see her granddaughter and, in her mind, hoped this would be a special party to reconnect her with her family.

Upon her eventual return to home from the hospital, the priest was invited for dinner when I was there one evening. He was not exactly an extrovert. She and I were burdened with carrying the strained conversation over dinner and it felt a little tense and uncomfortable. As steeped in church as I am, this should have been easy, but he had zero personality. I wondered, *How on earth does she even know this man?* By the end of the dinner, I still knew little to nothing about him, even how far away his church was. Once dessert was finished, he politely made his departure.

As Easter approached, I was struggling to feel the joy in the season. Alden was still unemployed. He had traveled to other branches of the glass manufacturing company he had worked for so many years with little resolution. After twenty-six and a half years and being very close to full retirement, this seemed so unfair. He could be employed in the California plant, but there was no way we could move from our little city of Shreveport. Our families were here and our friends were close by, as well as our church, and I really appreciated the jobs I had.

By now my mother had undergone many tests for excessive sleeping. The diagnosis came that we were not prepared for. It was cancer of the lymph glands. The doctors did not recommend that she undergo the severe radiation treatments. Instead, they suggested administering placebos and wanted to admit her to the hospital for the last stages of the disease. This would only treat her pain. It was so difficult to come to terms with and I refused to accept the diagnosis. Without telling her any details, we took her for a second opinion. Unfortunately, the results were the same. She had not lost weight and she did not look sick; this just did not seem right. The worry grew daily as I thought about this silent disease that had now found its way to my sweet mother. My sister and I decided not to tell her the diagnosis.

We knew it would only bring her a hopelessness that we could not bear her to feel. We tried to avoid talking about it. My dad, my sister, and I were in denial as she continued to do everything she always did as if she was not sick. Maybe the gift of not knowing, the gift of living each day as normal, would be what we could give her during this time. We chose to carry the dark secret that was ahead.

The Easter party preparations robbed me of my weekend time in the country with my parents. Alden, Melanie, and I went each weekend to the family farm and then back on Sunday morning for church. The drive back and forth was tiring, but the time was precious, especially being with my mother.

Easter Sunday, we attended church and went directly to Mrs. Winningham's Easter party. While I took my place in the office to answer some incoming phone calls, Melanie and Alden entertained themselves looking around the big beautiful mansion that had been so carefully decorated for the event. Melanie noticed the grand staircase. I had never been invited to tour upstairs so that was a bit of a mystery. Emmanuel took Melanie by the hand as her father followed behind to distract her while the eggs were being hidden on the back lawn.

The landscapers had done a great job! As an extra bonus, they had loaned her pink and white dogwood trees and placed them along the slope in the yard. It looked like a royal garden at Easter. Blooming flowers were everywhere, and there was every color and kind, all carefully placed in designs and coordinated to bring the wow factor! The large bunnies, chicks, and oversized Easter eggs scattered throughout the landscape were the icing on the cake.

The crowd arrived at 2:00 p.m. and as the house and yard began to fill up with children and adults, I had been given several excuses by Cora that Mrs. Winningham would come out of her room and join the party in another 30 minutes, and then another 30 minutes. I began to catch on to the stall tactics. More and more guests were arriving and still no appearance by the hostess. I asked to go in and help her, but she loudly ordered me to stay out. "Attend the party and watch the help! Keep your eyes on those six strangers in my kitchen," she said. She was unable to stand or walk. She sat in a chair, facing the windows and peered through the slightly opened shutters at her party taking place in the backyard—filled with people she did not know at a party she did not attend, even with all the grandeur and planning.

There was a crowd of people, all strangers, invited to partake in the beautiful landscaped lawn, delicious food and brightly colored eggs for the young ones to find. I did not see a child find a single egg or see the priest or even meet the families. I also did not see her the rest of the day. I paid all the workers with cash from her money bag, there for me to use when it was needed. She had told me to pay each of them $100 for their time and to be sure and watch them, so they did not walk off with her silver or a whole ham from the freezer. One of the staff did try that, but after I called the security guard, he returned the ham to the freezer.

The party seemed to be a success, I don't know how many attended, but the food had been eaten and the colorful punch polished off. I knew none of the guests, and not one of them told me thank you or that they enjoyed it as they left. My body was exhausted, and by 5:00 p.m., I was ready to go home.

Juggling both jobs, caring for Mrs. Winningham, and going to church on Wednesday nights for choir practice kept me quite busy, but I was keeping it together.

Mrs. Winningham had three trips in and out of the hospital during the summer and fall, each time going through the same process to detox her body from all the alcohol she consumed. Each time it took a little more of a toll on her.

Christmas was approaching, and she had plans for a pre-Christmas party. Two hundred engraved invitations were addressed and mailed. This was to be an adult-only party. The guest list included Presidents and Vice Presidents of several banks in town and top executives from every business. She meticulously chose not from a list of known business associates but from…. The Yellow Pages.

There was careful selection of decorators and designers to decorate the interior and exterior of her beautiful home. Yard lights were ordered from Dallas – cost was of no importance. The menu of food and drinks was fancy and extravagant. Helene, from Helene's Bar, was hired to sing and play the spectacular grand piano in the formal music room. There would also be dance music.

It was all orchestrated to be a dressy Who's Who affair. Again, I hired six people from the country club, waiters for the bar, valet service, and a security guard. The party would start at 8:00 p.m. but Alden and I arrived at 7:00 p.m. to ensure everything was in place and ready. Bonnie had arrived earlier to prepare Mrs. Winningham. She gave her a fresh hairdo, painted her beautiful nails, and dressed her in a long flowing shiny gown sent from a Dallas fashion house. Her shoes were covered with gold rhinestones. When I entered the room, she was lying on a velvet chaise in the music room with her glass in hand. She was happy that we had arrived early to help with the party.

Soon after we arrived, her friend, my boss, Charlie, arrived. Seeing her lying on the pink velvet chaise, he put out his hand and suggested they start the evening with a dance. She looked up at him and replied, "As soon as Helene starts playing music."

He smiled at her and said, "Will you play for us until she arrives."

With a slur in her response she said, "No, Charlie, I charge for my concerts." I could tell the words were difficult for her to form and within 45 minutes Emmanuel lifted her in his arms and carried her to her room. She was completely out and not aware that she had left the room before the party even began.

All the guests arrived and there was not one cancellation. The house was filled with people and the liquor flowed. Helene was singing humorous songs that kept the crowd laughing and entertained. Midway through the party, I noticed a young white couple coming in the front door. They looked very out of place. The young man was in a short-sleeved casual shirt and jeans with shoulder-length unkempt hair. The young woman had long black hair and was wearing jeans and a summer shirt that was untucked. In his arms a black baby was sleeping peacefully. The couple stood there silent, looking around the room at all the guests and the extravagant affair.

I called to Emmanuel. He came up behind me and, in a not-so-soft whisper, said, "My Gawd, that's Mr. Everett, her son. Dat's his wife and.... I don't know whose baby! They are not invited and sure gonna cause some trouble. Let me get Mr. Charlie to handle this."

As he quickly stepped away to find Charlie, I walked up to introduce myself as the person who had called him about the Easter party. He had nothing to say to me, just walked around the room enough to cause the Who's Who crowd to notice the mismatch of them with the black baby and their casual attire at such an elegant event. They did stand out for many reasons in that room of elite executives.

Charlie approached them and asked them to go out on the lawn to speak with him. It was only few minutes and he returned as they left.

I was so curious about what had just happened and why there was such distance between Mrs. Winningham and her son. I cornered my boss at the table and asked him to please help me understand why they did not speak. "What could have caused this much anger to create such distance between them?" I asked.

He sat down at the table and began the story. "When Mrs. Winningham's father, a well-to-do insurance executive, was alone and sick near the end of his life, he became very angry with her. She was his only child. His anger resulted in him cutting her out of his will. He passed his entire fortune to his grandson, Everett. That was about five years ago. Her father changed his will in the hospital just before he died. She took it to court against her son's wishes, of course, and recovered her inheritance. She tried to settle it by giving him a sizeable part of the money, but he wanted it all. It is true that she did not need the money, but she felt it was rightfully hers. He came here uninvited to embarrass her."

"Who does the child belong to?" I asked. "He told me it was theirs, but we can clearly see while it could be hers, it is not his baby." Then I asked, "Do you know Everett well enough to help mend the feud?"

Charlie looked me square in the eye and said, "Oh, yes, I have called him in my office and talked and talked, but he knows she is an alcoholic and he has no respect for her. She made him a spoiled brat as a kid by giving him everything, fancy cars and all the things he asked for or wanted. He is greedy and wants all the money. He has never had a job. She even bought him a house. She has sent him over $10,000 several times. His wife has been arrested for fooling around with the high school boys at the school near their house. When she hears about the black baby, I am sure she will binge again and end up in the hospital."

The party was over at midnight and Mrs. Winningham slept through it all. Alden and I left after everything had been cleaned up and the staff paid. The big beautiful house was once again quiet.

The following Monday evening while I worked at the big desk and Mrs. Winningham sat in her chair, after a very long and uncomfortable silence, she spoke. "I want you to know there is no black blood in my family or in Everett's father's family. I was a daughter of a blue-blooded Irishman. There is no way that is my son's child. It is hers and the man she slept with, which is obvious."

I nodded and said, "I agree. Had I known they were here sooner, I would have had Emmanuel throw them out."

Her speech was difficult to understand. I could see the effects of the strong drinks she was consuming, and I begged her to take care of herself. Christmas was very near, and I did not want to see her back in the hospital again. She asked if I would bring Melanie over to enjoy the decorations. She loved to see the delight in her eyes and watch her climb to the top of the stairs and slide down the banister. It gave her joy to see such awe and happiness in my young daughter's eyes. I am sure it made her think of the granddaughter she no longer got to see. A few days later, I did bring Melanie and we brought small gifts for Mrs. Winningham, Emmanuel, and Cora. I could tell this made her very happy.

She told me that a present had arrived in the mail from her son and she wanted me to open it. Her trembling hands removed the brown paper of a small box the size of a wallet. She seemed excited as I opened the small box and pulled out a grey flannel cloth that was made into a holder for eyeglasses. She told me that usually they were made of stiff materials to protect the glasses. This seemed like an unusual gift for him to give but I let her enjoy her moment of excitement.

Confused, Melanie whispered, "What is that for?"

Mrs. Winningham turned her attention to Melanie and begged for a hug. She quickly hugged and kissed her. It was in that brief moment that I could see the stiff layers of her veneer disappear. She loved her so completely; it was a feeling I knew she had not felt in some time. She asked Melanie to go slide down the banister one more time while she watched. The joy of something so small lifted her spirits more than I could imagine.

As Melanie reached the bottom of the stairs, she told her, "I have lots of work ahead for your mother. We will do a complete inventory of everything upstairs and down." I was pretty sure it was more about the company and future moments she could share with the two of us.

The inventory was done during the holidays, with appraisers coming in for all kinds of items. Only certified dealers made the appraisals. Some came as far away as Baton Rouge and they all came with outstanding reputations in their field.

This was very tiring for me at the holiday season, but it got her through Christmas without much idle time to feel alone and sad.

As I reflected back over the year, my personal books were balanced and thankfully we did not have to sell anything. I was grateful for this job and felt it was a blessing to my family and me. I wondered how long this pace would last and what the New Year would bring.

FIVE

*"At some point secrets become irrelevant.
The fact that you kept it does not."*
—Sara Gruen

It was a cool Sunday afternoon and New Year's Day had just passed. As I sat on the patio at my home, painting my nails, Alden sat nearby as we watched Melanie play with her new Christmas toys. While I was admiring my newly polished toes, I recalled the conversation I previously had with Brenda, the predecessor in my current position, when we had just met. She had quit her job to stay home with her husband and go barefoot. My feet could only breathe on Sunday afternoons and not until after 10:30 p.m. on week nights. Alden reached out to put my feet in his lap and lovingly massaged them. Maybe he too was thinking about those stockings and high heels that I wore so many hours a day. It had been an exhausting year, but we had made it through together.

Looking through the glass patio door into our home, I knew our beautiful holiday was over, and the Christmas decorations needed to be taken down. It was a true sign of packing away the last year and preparing for whatever was to come.

My thoughts were interrupted with Alden saying, "Hey Sugg, there is a chance of me getting a job at the Louisiana Ordinance Plant. I'm going to drive there tomorrow and check it out."

"That's great. Did you hear that they are hiring?"

"Yeah, I did. I'm not thrilled about the 40-mile drive every day, but if the money is good enough, I can do it." He lapsed back into his thoughts. I knew this had been hard on him. A man's job is directly connected to his confidence and self-worth. He was a strong, hardworking man and I prayed this new opportunity would be the one he needed.

He spoke up after several moments of silence, "We will need to change Melanie's school pickup."

I had already thought of that. "She can ride the bus from school to your mom's house. It is a short ride and she has a friend on the bus. She might even like that."

He replied with a sigh, "We will do what we have to do." My mother-in-law lived alone only a few minutes from us and since she had kept Melanie most of her preschool years, this would be an easy solution to our changing schedules.

"Speaking of Melanie's school," he said, "I forgot to tell you. Next Sunday afternoon a group of people are meeting at the Colvin's house to discuss building a private school not far from here. What do you think about going to see what it's all about? It is a group of parents like us that want a good education for their kids. I think we should check it out. It's a big undertaking, but I think if we are interested it would be good to be in at the beginning."

"Ok, put it on the calendar and we will go see what it's all about."

This had been such enjoyable time together talking and thinking about the things in our life. Our time was so rushed during the week; we needed this.

In the quiet time on the patio, I couldn't help but think of my mother and what was ahead. "Did you notice my mother didn't look so well yesterday? She thinks she has a bad heart. She has an appointment on Tuesday to see the doctor, and I plan on meeting her there to hear what he tells her."

"It's best that she thinks it's her heart rather than cancer; that would make her feel hopeless," he replied.

As the sun was setting over the backyard fence, we decided to call it a night and get some rest for the week ahead.

Monday, the first day back at the law office, I arrived ten minutes early to find my boss already there. I peeked into his office and could see the big vault door open. "Good morning, babe, come on in." I could see stacks of $100 bills in the vault and on the floor. "This big stash comes from the man across the way at the factory." He nodded towards the west. "It's for his black bastard son that comes in here each week for me to dole out to."

My eyes gazed at the loot as I said, "Wow, that should take care of him for life."

Barely phased by my wide-eyed comment, he replied, "Not hardly, I give him the rundown report the first of each year and he brings in the cash needed to take care of the boy for the coming year. This arrangement works for me and I think the man is happy too. I take my fees in cash and handle all the payments to keep things quiet around town." As he moved several bundles of cash to the side on the floor, he said, "If he thinks my fees are too high, I don't give a damn. I keep his good name intact."

"Sit down, dear, I feel chatty this morning, Did I ever tell you that I was once a U.S. Senator?"

"Oh, I have heard from Mrs. Winningham. She said that she knew you from her Washington days."

"Yep, I was there and served two terms. I liked it, but it was hard on my wife and children. Damn, every time I came home to Shreveport for a visit, my wife got pregnant. That's why I have five damn girls and one boy, that's a houseful."

He had told me most of this story before and it was a reminder that his gray hair was not premature but a sign of his aging, probably from a house full of squealing kids. He continued on with his story, "Yes, your gal-boss and I got to know Washington quite well and we made a few trips outside the country too. She was a beautiful gal in her heyday, had lots of classy friends, hob-knobbed with the wealthiest of people in Washington. Oh, and she enjoyed drinking good booze too—nothing but the finest. Her health was very good in those days. She thought she always had to have a man, and still does." He paused and gave a shrug and said, "Well, let's get to work."

This conversation had left me quite perplexed, but it gave me a much deeper understanding of Mrs. Winningham and the life that had led to her current situation.

Diane and I had worked to our maximum limit. All the quarterly reports had been filed, there were copies made and filed and I was closing out the books and preparing the 1099s. Mr. Crenshaw had his houseboy, their maid, Diane, and me on the payroll, and, of course, his monthly check, which was a big one!

Feeling the workload catching up with me, I needed a cup of coffee bad. Diane decided to go downstairs and bring back coffee for me and a juice for her. When she returned, my hand reached out for the coffee reminiscent of Mrs. Winningham reaching for her glass of hooch. I told Diane and she chuckled and said, "How I would love to see that house and that lady.... not to meet her, just see her without her knowing."

"Why don't you want to meet her?" I asked.
Diane replied, "Oh, gosh, she would intimidate me so much! I would be scared speechless; those kind of people make me nervous."

I laughed, "Are you kidding?"

"No, I'm not! Even here in the office, I couldn't handle these people that come in to meet with Mr. Crenshaw if you weren't here. It's just too terrifying, I don't know what to say to them."

"Diane, you never appear stressed and you handle everything and everyone perfectly."

"You just don't know what goes on inside my head. I

try to deal with it, but these well-educated, well-traveled people look at me and I feel so stupid. I have never been to college, except for business school right after high school, and then I got married." Her head was down, "I don't know how to talk to these people. I try to look busy or walk out of the office."

This was a newsflash to me. I had never imagined the insecurity going on inside her. "I'm sure you know how," I said, "Don't think like that. You are always so easy to talk to…."

She remained silent and just then, the boss entered the office and stopped short at my desk. He picked up my Styrofoam cup and drank the last few swallows of coffee.

"See you, girls, I'm off to the bank. Don't be drinking and partying while I'm gone."

"I can't stand these strict new guidelines, but this stack of statements will keep me out of trouble," said Diane with a smirk.

Mr. Crenshaw looked out of the corner of his eye and said with a grin, "My dear, we need to collect on those statements to keep our wheels turning." He picked up his hat and walked out the door, leaving us with a mountain of work.

Diane and I resumed our conversation once he was gone. Diane said, "Did I tell you what he said about my Christmas gift?"

"No, what did he give you?"

Looking rather disgusted, she said, "Nothing…. not money, not a card, not anything! He told me that he ordered a little something for my Christmas gift, but that it didn't come in. And then…he thanked me for the tie I gave him."

Suddenly I remembered the five $100 bills he had given me for Christmas that had come from his vault. The bonus I had never mentioned to Diane.

"Diane, I can't believe he is that stingy, that's awful." I didn't have the heart to tell her about the cash he had given me as a Christmas bonus. All I could do was listen with compassion and wonder why he would treat us so unequally.

Turning her chair back towards her typewriter, she said, "He's so tight he squeaks when he walks! That's why he won't buy his own cup of coffee. He's a stingy turd!"

We laughed out loud and agreed we would not work until he came back. We would just talk about our plans and a name for her baby that was due in June. It was our own secret revenge.

My husband was offered and accepted a job at the Louisiana Ordinance Plant. Melanie would ride the bus with her friend to her grandmother's house and he could pick her up after work. We were grateful for the paycheck and had managed to work out the logistics and schedules. We decided to celebrate over dinner and talk about our new beginning. Alden wanted me to decide soon which job I wanted to keep and quit the other one after our Christmas bills were paid. It had been a blessing to have both jobs and especially both paychecks, but I know it was also a sacrifice of our family time and precious time with my mother. I felt needed and appreciated at both, so the decision would not be simple.

Mrs. Winningham's bond coupons needed to be clipped at the bank again. I told her I would stop by the bank on my way from the law office and take care of them without her making a trip. She told me that she didn't plan on going back to the bank but since I was on her payroll, I should have Emmanuel take me in the limo whenever they needed to be clipped. After all, I represented her, and her household and I should go in style.

It was agreed that every three months Emmanuel, in his pristine chauffeur's attire, would drive me to the bank in first-class style to handle her business. He would usually have a cute non-alcoholic drink waiting for me. Once he even handed me a chilled coconut filled with fruit and a straw. He used those trips to apprise me of all that was going on at the mansion when I was not there.

He told me Mrs. Winningham was planning on having a guest that he deeply disliked. She was from Baton Rouge and had been there once before. He thought she was a distant relative and was the only relative he had ever heard about. I, too, knew of no relatives. There were never any Christmas cards, party invitations, or birthday cards for family. The list she had me send cards from were referred to as friends, not family.

News came from her plantation foreman that an oil and gas company had made a location to drill in one of the bean fields. She took the phone to address the foreman directly and said, "I did sign the lease giving them authority to drill, but you work out the land damage through my bookkeeper. As my plantation manager, you're too busy to leave your post to handle those affairs."

I guess she felt confident in me working out the details, knowing that I had previously worked for an oil company.

Within four weeks news came that the oil company had brought in a gusher of a well. I was excited for her and said, "That's wonderful, Mrs. Winningham, you are an oil tycoon."

With her drink in hand, she took a sip and with rigid body posture, she said, "Who cares? You have enough checks to take care of, don't you? All I can think of is another headache with taxes to be paid. If you were free to help me, we could spend some of it."

I choked under pressure and cleared my throat. She could literally go anywhere or do anything but she didn't want to go alone. All her money could not fill that void of being alone.

The awkward silence was broken as she said, "Tomorrow night, Charlie is coming for dinner. He wants duck, so that is what we will serve. Perhaps I can talk him into allowing you to leave the office early. I would like you to be here first to greet him and extend our welcome."

Slightly annoyed, I replied, "Tomorrow is Wednesday, I have choir practice at 7:00, so I would need to leave here by 6:45." She had tried many times in many ways before to get me to be there on Wednesdays. I knew this was a calculated move.

Then she said, shaking her head slowly up and down and watching me carefully for my reaction, "I understand you church people don't let many things get in your way of going to church."

"Well, Mrs. Winningham, I feel obligated to all the people in the choir. Some of them drive a long distance to be there. If I don't show up on a regular basis, I would be letting them down."

"Do you get paid?" she asked.

"Oh, no! No one is paid in the church except the pastor. I know God pays me in so many ways with all of his blessings."

She kept staring at me while I worked, perplexed by the thought of my commitment to something that she could not comprehend. My energy was running low as it had been a very busy day before I had even arrived there. I had gone with my mother to the doctor. The doctor had nothing more to say to her except, "Thank you for coming and I will see you again in another 30 days. Let me know if anything changes before then." He patted her on the back as we walked out. It was discouraging, to say the least. I kissed my mother and daddy and watched them drive off for their 70-mile trip home. I rushed back to the law office for another two hours of work before coming here. I was feeling the weight of the day and my energy level was dragging.

As Mrs. Winningham sat quietly across from me with my typewriter keys flying, I thought to myself, *The duck dinner doesn't particularly interest me. However, I am being paid to come and eat duck. How often does that happen?* And I knew how much it meant to her that I would be there, enough to pay me to do so. I decided to try and make it work, after all, I was grateful for both Mr. Crenshaw and her. How many other bosses would allow me to balance both jobs the way they did?

The next evening, Mr. Crenshaw allowed me to leave early as she had requested. Cora and Emmanuel had been preparing for our dinner most of the day. The table was set with her finest china and crystal and both were dressed in their pressed uniforms. The pre-requested duck was served under glass and all the trimmings were equally impressive. We kept the conversation light and our beautiful hostess seemed happy that we were both there. It could have been the pre-dinner beverages she consumed, but I know she was happy to have the company and even though I had to rush out at 6:45 p.m. to make it to choir practice, she didn't seem to be bothered.

My husband supposed his job would be tolerable, at least for a while. His paycheck was decent, better than the unemployment benefits he had been getting. It was at least a temporary fix until something better came along. After some discussion, we decided to buy $500 in school bonds and had agreed to help build the private school. The group of families that had come together was nothing short of a miracle. Most were middle-class families that just wanted a better option and control in our children's education. There were many tradesmen who worked tirelessly after their full day of work to do things like plumbing, electrical, and painting. My mother-in-law kept Melanie until 9:30 or 10:00 p.m. to allow Alden to lend a hand after his work hours and his 40-mile drive back to town. It was truly the efforts and hard work of all the parents that would build this school. It was by the sacrifices of many that it all came together in a relatively short time. The school was scheduled to open at the end of August and it was located only three miles from our house. That would make mornings easy.

Mr. Crenshaw became ill and didn't make it into the office for two weeks. Diane and I had nice long lunches to shop for spring clothes and things for the new baby. Diane had secretly planned to leave her job at the end of March to allow two months to rest before her little Jennifer would be born. My plan was not so clear yet. *Which job would I leave?* I knew Mrs. Winningham depended on me for so much, but then the law office would be losing Diane. It was a difficult decision. I really missed the benefits and amenities of my last job. There was no insurance or retirement at either of the jobs.

Diane and I handled several transactions without the boss. We had daily contact with him for any questions we might have. We closed home mortgages and many other tasks without the help of the boss. We were quite the team. I knew I was going to miss her.

Over at the mansion, Emmanuel and Cora were preparing for the guest to arrive. Mrs. Winningham had not mentioned a guest to me. They told me she planned to have a bridge party on Wednesday afternoon, my night off. The staff was put on notice to work until the party was over, but no specific time was given. They loved to fill me in on the little secrets when she was down the hall in the bathroom.

Mrs. Winningham's spring wardrobe had arrived from Dallas. It was absolutely gorgeous! She had exquisite taste. Emmanuel had driven her to Goldring's, a very high-end clothing boutique. She sent him inside with a blouse, a suit, and a dress for them to accessorize, then bring everything back to the limo for her approval. I can only imagine the looks, this large black man dressed in his chauffeur's attire, carrying in her wardrobe collection and asking for the latest in earrings and bling to match the outfits received. That is what you call real curb service!

The following Thursday evening, I was served dinner at the table alone. As Cora served me, she said that Emmanuel was resting in his quarters and that Mrs. Winningham and her guest were in their rooms sleeping. I could tell there was a slight hesitation in her voice. It was very abnormal for him not to greet me at the door as he usually did. I asked how the bridge party went. She filled my glass of tea and said with a roll of her eyes that Emmanuel would fill me in later. After I finished dinner, I made my way down the hall to the office to address the stack of papers and bills waiting on my desk. As I passed the staircase, I saw a man dressed in a suit with a suitcase in one hand and carrying a hat in the other. He made no eye contact with me and swiftly made his way to the front door.

It was 9:00 p.m. before Emmanuel came into the office and slumped into the big chair.

"Emmanuel, I am glad you came in. How did the bridge game go?" I asked. "Earlier I saw a man come down the stairs with a piece of luggage. He didn't speak a word to me, just walked fast through the living room and out the front door. I didn't even notice a car here."

He rolled his dark eyes and said, "I guess he called a cab."

"Do you know him? He was about 45 years old and quite handsome."

"No, no, I don't know him; he's just somebody *they* called."

There was a moment of silence and no more details. Not wanting to pry, I thought it best to change the subject. "Emmanuel, how did the bridge party turn out?"

"Oh Gawd, you'll see, that's what I came to tell you, I have had it with this job. I'm getting too old to be kept awake every night. I have no benefits and will not be able to draw a retirement from her as it is. This is just too much! I am hoping you can talk to her about this. I just can't. You will need to catch her at a good time—and that is not going to be tonight.

"Sure, I'll be glad to discuss it with her. It's time for you to get a raise. You haven't had one since I have been here." I thought the hope of more money would perk him up, but it didn't seem to lighten his mood.

"I think you need to see in the rooms where they are. Gawd, I can't go in there tonight and get her ready for bed. I think I will quit first."

Not sure what was so bad that put him to the point of quitting and quite confused about what it had to do with the bridge game or who was the "they" he was referring to, I followed him down the long hallway to Mrs. Winningham's bedroom door.

I looked at him, unsure what he wanted me to do. I said, "I'll knock on the door." I had been in her bedroom only a handful of times before. The last time was the day of the Easter party and she had made me feel uneasy and out of place on that day. I knocked twice but there was no answer. I turned the knob and eased the door ajar to peek inside. I saw her on the bed ... lying unresponsive there in all her glory ... totally nude. Relieved I could see she was breathing, I pushed the door wider for a better view of the room. It was in total shambles! The bedside lamp had been smashed on the floor, glass was everywhere, and the mirrors were broken. It looked like everything that was breakable was in a million pieces.

I pulled the door quietly closed and returned to Emmanuel waiting in the hall. At the look of shock on my face, contemplating what to do or say next, he said, "You didn't look in at Miss Fern's room, did ya? There is some more of the same in there, and we ain't gonna worry about putting her to bed."

I was busy processing all that I had just seen and even more of what the scene must have been like before I arrived. Poor Emmanuel, I could tell he was hanging by his last thread and had probably dealt with this more times that I could have imagined.

With the thought of Mrs. Winningham waking up and trying to get to the bathroom in the night, I knew I needed to do something. I asked Emmanuel to go get a broom and dustpan and I would go in and try to get her to the bathroom and in her night clothes.

Emmanuel said, "She will be angry at the sight of me, but she won't you. Just look in her closet for them night clothes."

I rolled up my sleeves and headed into the room. Stepping carefully in my high heels around the broken objects, I swept a path from her bed to the bathroom, ran a tub of water, and poured in a floral fragrance from the side of the tub. There were many beautiful gowns and robes in her expansive closet, so I made a selection and walked back to her bedside.

All the noise I made had not awakened her at all. I spread the robe over her naked body. She was lying on her side, so I slipped one arm in the sleeve and as I rolled her to her other side she moaned an "Oh!" She was in such a drunken stupor that even as I called her name in a firm tone to tell her we were going to the bathroom, she didn't seem to care. She held out a trembling hand towards me to help her pull upright. Sitting on the side of the bed, she started to attempt to push her hair back into place as if that was the irregular part of this situation. Somehow, her less-than-perfect hairdo was the last thing I was going to remember from this night of firsts. Again, with a firm voice, I told her to get up, we were going to the bathroom. Her legs would barely support her, but she shuffled along, holding on to me.

When the door closed to the bathroom, I could hear Emmanuel in the bedroom with a garbage can, throwing all the broken treasures away. Then the loud vacuum cleaner noise with all the broken bits clattering as it sucked away the wreckage of the evening, at least the visual reminders.

After I helped her step into the huge marble tub with all the jets swirling the water, I handed her a sponge for her to proceed with her own bath. I sat down in a blue silk-covered chair near the tub. What a lavish feeling it must be to have an extravagant tub like this, with its gold fixtures, surrounded by greenery and flowers and candles that smelled wonderful.

No words were spoken as I began looking at my manicure and checking my teeth in her ornate hand mirror on the vanity. As I sat there in silence thinking about this night, and the high probability of so many others I knew nothing of, it occurred to me that Cora left each night after cleaning the kitchen, once dinner was complete. The reality was pretty clear—Emmanuel had been doing this drunken bedtime process all along by himself. He weighed about 350 lbs. and was not a physically fit man.

I inconspicuously glanced at her nude body in the tub. She was still a work of art, a truly beautiful woman. Her skin was porcelain perfect and with all the personal attention Bonnie, the beautician, gave her on a regular basis it was no wonder. Her breasts were a perfect "D" cup and did not sag at all like you would expect for a woman of her age. But, then again, as she had said, "Money can get you anything." She was certainly vain enough and would only have seen the very best of doctors to keep everything tucked and lifted.

Once the noise had stopped in the bedroom, I peeked through the door to see Emmanuel leaving with the dirty sheets under his arm. He had put fresh silk sheets and pillowcases on her bed with a blue silky crepe comforter.

I turned and picked up a towel as I raised my voice to get her attention, "Are you ready to get out? Your bed and room are ready."

She managed to mutter, "Ok."

She told me the color of night clothes she wanted. I thought, *Her head must be pounding and here she is telling me she wants a particular color of nightgown.*

When I had her tucked in bed, she said a very sheepish, "Thank you, will you tell Emmanuel to come in? I am very thirsty."

"Mrs. Winningham, I'll come back tomorrow for a couple hours of work." I needed to handle something for Emmanuel.

"Sure, sure, I think my guest is leaving on Saturday," she replied.

I said good night and turned on my heels to head for my car. Emmanuel was standing outside the front door and watched me as I walked to the car.

I said, "Sleep well tonight. Tomorrow I'll get you that raise and discuss a retirement plan." In my head I was thinking, *Surely, he can't leave her before I do, but boy, if this is what he goes through on a regular basis, he surely needs a raise!*

On Friday when I returned, I met the house guest, Miss Fern. Not quite as well-preserved as her friend, the effects of the hooch on her was showing. However, she was well groomed, intelligent, attractive and obviously belonged to the jet set group. She said she would be flying to New

York on Saturday. She had stopped off in Shreveport to see her friend and play a hand of bridge. She failed to mention the numerous cocktails she and her friend had also enjoyed and there was no mention of the broken lamps, vases, mirrors and other priceless treasures. There was also no mention of the man who had made his exit down the stairs and his silent departure to escape the chaos. He must have been a part of the bedlam. I have heard of drunken brawls, but this one was hard to imagine in a house like this.

Emmanuel was very happy with the raise and retirement plan I had gotten for him. It assured him that he would be able to retire with almost his same paycheck when the time came. Mrs. Winningham agreed to the changes without much convincing. I think she realized all he did for her and was grateful for the things he did to take care of her so many times.

A week later, Mrs. Winningham was back in the hospital for another five days. I guess it was no surprise and the pattern of all the times before was much clearer now.

My mother's health was declining quickly, and this was weighing on my mind. I was also missing the college classes I had put on hold. Alden encouraged me to take off and check out the class schedules and give one boss or the other my notice. It was either leaving or taking the time off for my classes, as simple as that.

SIX

"Our only security is our ability to change."
—John Lilly

It was a cold Monday morning in February, and Mr. Crenshaw had not arrived at the law offices. Diane and I were chatting fast about our weekends to get in all the details. I told her that while reading the newspaper on Sunday, I saw an ad for a bookkeeper/executive secretary and the salary was $5,000 a month. The ad was really large and caught my eye since it mentioned oil and gas experience was required. Diane said, "Go for it! Send your resume in today!"

"That is a lot of money, do you really think I can qualify for it?"

"Sure, you can!"

Still doubtful, and more out of the novelty of it, I ate my sandwich and drank a Coke at my desk during lunch to type my resume. Not taking it too seriously, but liking the challenge, I mailed my resume to the address in the newspaper.

The following Wednesday I ran by the college to pick up a class schedule before going home for a quick dinner. Choir practice would be at 7:00 p.m. so I was on a tight timeline. When I made it home, Alden met me at the door with a phone number on a piece of paper. He had told the gentleman who called that I had gone to school, but he would have me return the call later that evening. Alden seemed disturbed and a bit baffled at the situation since he was unaware that I had submitted my resume.

I sat down to collect myself, made sure the household was quiet and returned the call at 5:15 p.m. The voice on the other end of the phone was very distinguished. He told me I had been selected as one of three to be interviewed for the position. He knew my boss, Charlie, as he was known around town. He promised he would keep the interview confidential as to not jeopardize my current job if I was not offered the new one. He told me he was impressed that I was continuing my education. The interview was set for the following day, Thursday, at noon.

I was very flattered, but still did not give much credence to the possibility. All I had to lose was a lunch hour. I had not given a lot of thought to really changing jobs, only giving up one of the two I had.

The next morning, I put on my newest suit and heels. I felt pretty good as I made my way to the law office. Diane was all smiles and excited about the interview. The interview was in the building just across the street on the 17th floor. She walked with me to the building entrance and wished me luck, assuring me that no one would ever know about the interview except us.

When I entered the McCormick-Jordan Oil & Gas Office, a pretty blonde receptionist was there to greet me and introduce me to the boss. "He's expecting you," she said, as she walked me down the hall.

There was not much time to take in my surroundings, but everything looked first class. The furniture was fine wood, there was plush light blue carpet and a glass curio cabinet that held a collection of what looked to be expensive mineral stones. A cluster of office doors opened to the reception area. The doors were ajar, enough to see the oversized windows that overlooked the city and the river winding between the two cities of Shreveport and Bossier.

The receptionist did not take long to announce my arrival and summoned me into the ultra-modern office of Mr. Reed T. McCormick. He was a man in his sixties with blonde hair, wearing a white shirt with a colorful silk ascot at the neck. This was a completely new look to me; no one around town dressed like this. He apologized for not wearing his suit jacket; it was draped over the sofa in the office. I paused a minute to take in the room and all its grandeur. His massive oak desk was carved and there were two very tall black leather chairs. There was a glass table with green plants around the room and a TV in his office. His office was much larger than the attorney's offices. A conference room with a long table and many chairs adjoined his office. Geological logs were spread out on his desk as though he had been examining the formations prior to my arrival.

I was surprisingly at ease as I settled into the big leather chair across from him. I looked straight into his very blue eyes. I was certain that it was likely that I was competing for the job against two men, since many accountants and bookkeepers were men, but at least I would get experience in interviewing and have a good story to tell Diane.

Mr. McCormick informed me that he was the senior partner. He and his young partner/protégé, Henry Jordan, were very proud of what they had accomplished together. The Shreveport office had five employees and they had opened a second office two years ago in Lafayette with a staff of four. Jackson, Mississippi, was their most recent office to launch.

As he leaned forward across his desk, he said, "I'm offering a healthy salary to the right person, with paid vacation, health and life insurance. I expect the person that fills this role to know about everything and everyone and report directly to me by phone. I spend the summers in my Canada home, and I have a plane and a pilot to make trips back and forth as necessary."

He reached for his phone and buzzed the receptionist to bring in one of the ledger books so that I could see their system. I had not kept books by a voucher system before, but I was able to understand, and it seemed to be an efficient way to keep monthly paid receipts. The system had been set up by his personal secretary many years ago, before she got too bossy, at which time he "asked her to retire." He said, "She was too damn hard to get along with." He added, "I believe someone smart could do better learning the bookkeeping system without her help. I'm sure the CPA will be glad to help if we run into problems."

I carefully examined the postings and her beautiful handwriting. Every sheet was meticulously done without one single correction on the pages. There was payroll to keep, checks to sign, and most importantly, keep money transferred to his Canada account as needed.

"Now, how do things look to you so far, Mrs. Marsh?" Hearing him call my name and interrupting my thoughts of the tasks he had described was a bit startling. I stammered a bit as I replied, "The bookkeeping was the fun part of all my jobs in the past; I really enjoy that. My shorthand is not so fast until I am more familiar with the terminology and your specific vocabulary, but I do have oil and gas experience."

"I saw on your resume that you had worked for Mr. Roth. I knew him from past oil deals and we played a few rounds of golf together. He was a good golfer, a good geologist, and a very good man. I'm sure sorry we lost him."

He cleared his throat and sat up, rolling his chair close to the desk and leaning forward. "Now, Mrs. Marsh, I have saved something until last to spring on you about this job. I doubt you or anyone in Shreveport will have had this experience. I am looking for someone I can trust, who is dependable, courageous, and mature enough to understand the responsibility that I will entrust them with in this role. Recently, I purchased a 110' yacht with a crew of five, a captain, a cook and three deck hands. The captain put the crew together; they need to be compatible. They are all very British. You will soon discover that I don't know what the hell I am doing in the yacht business. I plan to let others charter the yacht during the months I am not using it. It is presently chartered by two people for two months, cruising the Caribbean. After that, it will be brought to the harbor off the coast of Florida for the cleanup, redecorating, and restocking. They will send the paperwork to this office, receive the payroll, and take on the next charter. It is booked out for the next six months. I will give advice, but really don't want the day-to-day worries. I understand yachts that are chartered need to be redecorated often to keep them appealing and new. A decorator has to come in and rip it all down and bring in a new look. I have not chartered before, but to own a yacht is the most exciting thing I've ever done with my pants on."

I think he said that for shock factor to loosen up my frozen expression. All of this was mind-boggling.

After a brief pause he continued, "My summer home is in Canada on an island. I own the island and this summer and spring when the ice thaws, I will spend some time making some improvements and doing a bit of entertaining with some friends. Once they leave, my four sons and their families fly up for two weeks. Their homes and businesses are in Houston and Dallas. We try to get in a little fishing in the Canadian waters when we are together. I have a small seaplane to get us around there."

He walked towards a very large impressive framed picture on the wall of land and water and motioned for me to follow. He pointed to the aerial view of the island, "Here is the mainland. We travel by boat or the seaplane for all our supplies and to get the mail in the warm months. In the winter, the water is frozen solid and everything on the island has to be winterized until the next thaw in the spring. We hire some local people to come clean and reassemble everything to be ready for our move back in the spring."

"It must be beautiful."

"Yeah, wish you could see it." He looked down at his expensive watch. "I have taken your lunch hour and about ten minutes of Charlie's time. Tell him you are taking care of business if he gives you a hard time."

I could hear the voices of the employees as they returned from lunch.

"Thank you, Mrs. Marsh, for coming in to see me today. I'll be making my decision in a day or two." He walked me to the reception area and reached out his hand.

"Thank you, Mr. McCormick, I appreciate your time."

My mind was racing as I stepped onto the elevator. When it reached the ground floor of the building, I dashed back towards my office. I could not wait to tell Diane everything. The boss was at the courthouse, so I talked as fast as I could, telling her all the details of this fairy tale life I had just heard.

"**O**h well, it was just an interview. I am certain the job will go to a man, it's a management-type position," I said.

Diane mumbled, "It's strange how the opening came up at a time you could not be more stretched between two jobs."

"I can at least say the interview was an exciting experience."

We focused on our work and slaved over our typewriters all afternoon. Several hours had passed. I was still thinking about the interview and broke the silence with a sigh and said, "Diane, wouldn't that be a great paycheck?"

"Yes, and just think you wouldn't have to share your coffee or keep up with his hat, coat, and umbrella. I know you can handle the job if you get the opportunity. Just think positive."

At the end of the day, I headed for Mrs. Winningham's where she had the usual load of work waiting for me after we finished dinner. She nodded her head as she listened to my chatter about my family, barely picking at her food.

"Everyone must have a birthday in February. Just look at how many cards we have to address," I said after dinner.

She sat watching me with the large diamond ring flashing on her beautiful hands with her red polished nails.

"Emmanuel puts less and less in my glass." She pursed her lips and stretched her eyes. "He can just get himself up and make more trips to get me more. "She pressed the buzzer next to her and called for Emmanuel.

When she got up to go to the bathroom, Emmanuel sat down across from me and said, "I sincerely want to thank you for helping me get the pay raise and the retirement benefits."

I told him I didn't have any problem getting her to agree, she was very willing. The retirement would begin at her death or his failure in health or disability. He would draw three-fourths of his salary along with any Social Security benefits.

"I'll always be grateful to you, Mrs. Marsh. It means a lot."

I could see the gratitude in his eyes and I knew he had more than earned every penny and more. "You are welcome, Emmanuel, enough said. It is in writing, signed, and notarized by me and witnessed by Cora and Charlie. That business is finished. Now we just need to get this lady healthy. That is the hurdle I see."

"We are far too late for that," he said. "She ain't gonna let nobody change her. I don't think she has an interest in anything anymore. She stopped watching television and reading books and newspapers. Ever since the brawl, she has been drinking steadily."

"Then we know where she is headed," I said.

"Gawd, I dread those hospital trips," he muttered.

We stopped our conversation as he heard her coming down the hall. She walked slowly with one hand on the wall to steady her balance. Emmanuel met her halfway with his left arm around her and his right arm out for her to hold. She straightened herself into the regal stance she liked to maintain, looking at me as she walked towards her chair. Her signatures on the checks were barely legible. She blamed the pen for her struggles and asked me to please finish signing them for her. When all was complete, I neatened the desk and told her, "Good night."

When I arrived home, I told Alden and Melanie the story of my unusual interview. My husband's summation of why I did the interview was a diversion to escape my big load of problems. He thought the job seemed a little farfetched.

A few days later, Mrs. Winningham was hospitalized again. I hired nurses to cover the shifts around the clock. Emmanuel and I were well practiced at this routine and took care of all the duties by her side.

That night at 9:00 p.m., the phone rang. It was Mr. McCormick. He said he was determined to catch me, even if it was midnight. He had reached his decision from the three interviews and would like me to please come to his office at noon to discuss a starting date. "I need you as soon as possible."

"Thank you, Mr. McCormick, I'll see you at noon." I could hardly believe what I had just heard. *How could this possibly work out? Where do I begin? Mrs. Winningham is still in the hospital and I would rather not tell the new boss about that,* I pondered.

Mr. McCormick told me I would have a secretary, the receptionist. She would take care of all my correspondence, typing, and any work I would delegate. Any help I needed, she would take care of. He would only be in the office one month to handle any details that needed his attention before leaving for Canada.

The office hours were from 8:30 a.m. to 5:00 p.m., but on the days he was in town he chose to get there by 10:00 a.m. It would be up to me to get the jobs done without having to punch a time clock.

I made the decision to give two weeks' notice at the

law office. If it was absolutely necessary, I could stay two weeks, but it would be better for my new position if they would accept one week.

When I returned to the law office, I went straight to Mr. Crenshaw's office and settled in a chair to wait for his return from lunch. Diane had been waiting to see my answer and, in a flash, she had gone from happy to sad thinking of the reality of us not being together. She said it was like a death. I promised to have lunch with her every day that I could until she left the law office in March.

Mr. Crenshaw accepted the news well. He said it was unusual that I had kept the job for two years. He usually rotated secretaries every three to six months because there were no benefits other than the short hours. He told me that without someone taking care of the details as well as we had done, he would have to reschedule taking caseloads. It was long overdue for him to taper down his business.

I could feel myself starting to cry and then audibly sobbing.

"Please don't cry," he said. "I want you to climb higher in your career than this. Maybe if I were younger, I could spread some more excitement around in this job, but it's time. Just grab the job and go for it! I will help you in any way I can. We will always remain friends!"

"That means everything." I dried my eyes and sat quietly for a minute. "What should I do about Mrs. Winningham?"

"Handle that day by day. That is your after-work job. McCormick won't be concerned with what you do for her after hours. It's simple: STOP WORRYING!"

SEVEN

"Those who cannot remember the past are condemned to repeat it."
—George Santayana

The new job began on Monday. With all the new faces around me, I felt like everyone was watching me, waiting to see the smart kick in from somewhere. Everyone was warm and friendly, except the grey-haired lady who was in her sixties and seemed to be staying away from me. The receptionist was a fast typist and eager to please me and be helpful. She even served me coffee, a big difference from having Mr. Crenshaw drink the one I bought for myself each morning. I felt really good about the new job and the decision I had made.

By Wednesday noon, I made a visit to the hospital to check on Mrs. Winningham. The physician told me they were making arrangements to fly her to Houston.

"Those boys can try and turn her around, because we can't do any more," he said.

My voice trembled as I asked, "Do you mean you think she won't come out of this coma?"

"Nothing we have tried is working this time. It's that dreaded time that we had hoped would not come. I suggest you call her next of kin. We are lining up the trip for this afternoon. The quicker we can get her there, the more time they will have to do whatever can be done at this point."

Emmanuel and I stood there looking at each other, feeling the gravity of what was next. "Emmanuel, you will need to fly with her there, I can't leave. I will take care of the money issues and call Mr. Crenshaw. He can call her son or be responsible for not calling him."

Emmanuel interrupted, "It ain't gonna do no good to call him, he don't care one way or the other."

The airlift was arranged quickly to get her to Houston with Emmanuel by her side. He kept me posted as she grew steadily worse each day.

The following Monday, Mr. Crenshaw had gone to Houston to check on her. He called me at 6:00 p.m. to tell me that Emmanuel and he would be returning to Shreveport with her body. She had not responded to the treatment and she had passed. Mr. Crenshaw asked me to help him put together the funeral arrangements and if he needed to speak to McCormick to allow me to complete some business, he would.

Mrs. Winningham had prearranged the music for her service. I called the Catholic priest from the Easter event, but since she was not a member of his congregation, he thought it best to get someone else. Mr. Crenshaw asked his minister to handle the service. He was to arrange for her pallbearers among the friends she knew. He said, "It was difficult to find four other men besides Emmanuel and me. I thought I would have to hire someone. I know damn well the four I got don't know who the hell she is, but that's all I can do."

The service would be at the funeral home chapel, but a graveside service would have been better. There were only two rows used to seat people who attended, even with the pallbearers. There was a single song selected, *Going Home*. She had lived an elegant but lonely life.

Mr. Crenshaw, Emmanuel, Cora, my family, and I rode the 30 miles together for the burial. The four friends of Mr. Crenshaw's, the pallbearers, followed behind us. The minister rode in the hearse with the driver and her body.

Everett had told Mr. Crenshaw he would meet him at the cemetery, but when we arrived, he was not there. We waited for half an hour sitting in the cars, but still he was a no-show. The body was carried to the burial site and placed ready for the last words and prayer. Another half hour passed, and he was still not there. The minister began.

Halfway through the prayer we heard two people coming through the gate laughing and talking as if this occasion was something other than somber. They continued walking up to the small group. The minister did not pause but continued with his prayer.

Mr. Crenshaw leaned over and asked Everett and his wife why they were delayed.

His reply was one we had not anticipated, "We stopped for lunch before we came, it took a little longer than we thought. Guess it made us late, huh?" The lack of respect and complete indifference to having us wait to bury his mother while he and his wife had a leisurely lunch was enough to make my blood boil.

Mr. Crenshaw leaned towards me and said, "I guess one excuse is as good as another."

It was a total disgrace to this lady of grace. Although her flaws were on display at the end of her life, I felt certain there was much more to the beautiful queen of the mansion. I had been her friend and knew her in a way no one else would.

As our small group made our way to the car for the journey home, Mr. Crenshaw promised that the probation of her will would not happen until Everett was too old to enjoy it. He would see to that personally.

The quote Mrs. Winningham had said on occasion came racing back to my thoughts.

"Those who do not learn from history are condemned to repeat it."

New locks were put on every door of the mansion, and the bank accounts were sealed awaiting the probate of the will. Emmanuel moved out of the garage apartment and the grand mansion sat dark, still, and lifeless. I could imagine the big majestic house that had once greeted important guests and hosted parties, the secrets it held behind the big beautiful doors, and the facade of grandeur now dimmed. The fine china and crystal were left on the shelves, the collections of a lifetime of world travels and elegance left in the dark loneliness. In the weeks that followed, I was often brought back to that stillness and thoughts of the secret life of the grande dame and of the parties she watched from her room. There must have been great pain in her past that she tried to numb with the contents of those beautiful crystal glasses. I hoped she had found peace.

The shock came one month from the day of the funeral. Mr. Crenshaw called and said, "Take a look at the newspaper! Everett shot and killed his wife last night! The children were away visiting, and he shot her! Yes, he shot her! It is reported as an accidental shooting." The tone in his voice let me know he didn't believe that for a minute.

The newspaper said that Everett was cleaning his hunting rifle in the bedroom while she was in bed. The gun went off, hitting her in the head. Only the two of them were in the house at the time.

This was a lot to swallow! His wealthy mother, who he showed no outward emotional attachment to, died and 30 days later, his cheating wife is accidentally shot while the children were away from home? There were a lot of gaps in the story and no one seemed to be asking questions. It was simply filed as an accident and no one raised an eyebrow.

Two days later, I made the trip to the funeral home during my lunch hour. There were only two visitors there—her adopted parents who lived out of town. The loss of a child would be horrific for any parent. I told them I was sorry for their loss.

Her mother replied, "Don't feel sorry for us. She has lived a rebellious life for 25 years. You just can't imagine the things she has done and the anxiety she has created.

If he said it was an accident, we believe him, and we forgive him. We think she and Everett were two of a kind, cut from the same cloth. Neither of them ever had a job. There was no motivating them, they just expected others to give them everything and felt entitled to whatever they wanted. It was not the life we would have chosen for her, but she was defiant and did not want anything different."

The mood was somber and with no one there, I could tell she did not spend her life making friends, and as cold as it was, she would not be missed by many.

They thanked me for coming and for listening. I hugged both of them and headed back to the office. It was an uncomfortable and awkward situation, but I was glad I had gone to pay my respects to her parents. They had lost a daughter and that was worth empathy and respect.

Sadly, the young black baby boy was never mentioned or seen again. No questions were asked, and the case was closed with the accidental shooting listed as the cause of death. I remember the words Mrs. Winningham said to me, "If you have money, you can buy anything."

Back at the new office, there was plenty of work waiting for me. Keeping up with the meticulous bookkeeping I had been left with was ongoing and took daily maintenance. Mr. McCormick usually stayed on the phone or left the office during the day. There was a lot for me to learn, most especially when it came to management of a yacht, but I embraced the changes and felt confident in my new role in no time at all. The day-to-day functions and my familiarity with the oil and gas business helped me to gain Mr. McCormick's trust quickly. He depended on me, and I liked that.

Sitting at my desk one morning, I intercepted a phone call for Mr. McCormick. Without identifying herself, the woman on the phone asked to speak to my boss saying, "Could you tell him he has a call from Canada?" I placed the call on hold and walked into his office. He shook his head and gestured for me to put the call through, then asked that I close his office door. I resumed sorting through the pile of work on my desk and didn't think much more of it. I was feeling pretty lucky to have landed such a great job; my first paycheck made me truly happy!

Several weeks had passed quickly and it was time for Mr. McCormick to return to Canada. Preparation for his departure took a few days and there were business issues to be handled. Uncertain how long he would be away, I knew I needed to have a good grasp on things to be able to accomplish my task without him there. Making my way through the stacks and files on my desk helped give me a good start to finding my own way and understanding what I would be responsible for in this new position.

Again, there was another call from the mysterious lady from Canada. By now I came to recognize this meant for me to close the door for privacy. I guessed it was some big secret business deal or perhaps someone taking care of his property in Canada.

Later that day, he called me into his office. As I sat in the chair across from his desk, he stood with his back to me, facing the big windows that looked out over the city. I waited with my pen and paper in hand for the reason he had called me in. Finally he said, "Mrs. Marsh, you are a Christian, right? Do you believe we all have a secret corner within us, a small place that we have private to ourself?"

I could tell he was in deep thought and I wasn't sure how to respond to a question like that. I had never been asked something like that, especially from my boss. So, I took a deep breath and gave him the most honest answer I could. "I think God is a part of all the little corners of who we are and he knows all our secrets. I'm not sure if that is the answer you were looking for, but it is what I believe."

Still gazing out the window, he replied in a soft voice, "Ok, thank you." His mood was somber, and I could tell there was much more to the question than he had revealed. I'm not sure what brought on that moment of sincerity and questioning, but I'm glad he trusted me enough to talk. He obviously trusted me a great deal to leave me with such big responsibilities for months at a time: to take care of his yacht, the ins and outs of his bookkeeping, all the details of the day-to-day business without looking over my shoulder. Yes, he trusted me, and I respected him for treating me with such total trust and generosity.

I remembered the day he entrusted me with a personal story, one that is both sad and funny. He said, "Mrs. Marsh, you might find this story interesting. About two years ago, I spent a whole damn year and tons of money on a thousand acres that I bought just outside of Shreveport. It was beautiful and out in the middle of nowhere. I purchased it with the intent to clean it up, make it a real showplace, and give it as a surprise gift to my four grown sons. I hired crews of heavy equipment operators who worked every day cleaning and clearing the underbrush and manicuring every detail of the property. Hell, we even came up on a damn cemetery on the property that we didn't know was there. It was old, I mean, really, really old! It had about a dozen graves and most of the tombstones were broken and falling down. I got into all kinds of legal trouble over that. We couldn't locate any living relatives and I ended up having to buy some additional property and have them all moved.

"That took months! What an ordeal it turned into. After that fiasco, I hired all kinds of tree and landscape experts to choose the trees to save and to design the terrain. There were streams with bridges arching over them and two large ponds stocked with fish. It had a blacktop road that wound throughout the property with big beautiful iron gates that anchored the entrance. It was a lot of work and a full year of pouring into the details of this stunning place that was to be my prize gift to the boys. It was a true Garden of Eden, a 1,000-acre oasis that I was so proud of.

"The day finally came for the big reveal. I invited all four of the boys to fly into the Shreveport airport at 7:00 a.m. I asked them to dress in suits appropriate for pictures. I got my driver to rent a big luxury van. We met them at the airport and had breakfast before heading for the immense surprise down the road. The two boys in the middle seat turned around to face the two boys in the back seat and one let out a big loud fart! Of course, this started uncontrollable laughter between them and then they started the 'trumping game,' which one could out fart the other one. They acted just like they did when they were little kids. I tried to get them to quiet down and act like the grown men they were, but that only made them laugh harder. When they ran out of real farts, they started putting their hands under their armpits and kept the game going. They were laughing, but I was not. This was the day I had worked for and planned for and they were more interested in playing the fart game.

"When we finally reached the grand front gates, I had the driver stop. We all got out to take a picture of the four boys by the entrance. They didn't say a word, not one question even. They got out and posed for the picture as if they had been there many times before. We all got back in the fancy rented van and rode to the top of the hill for the breathtaking view of the vast, manicured culmination of the yearlong project. There was not a word as they looked out over the place, until one spoke up and said, 'Hey, if we had only brought our guns, I bet we could have sacked us some of the wildlife.' Little did they know the wildlife had been carefully picked and protected by high fences.

"There was no other conversation, not one word about the beauty or the miraculous estate they were standing on. Not even one out of the four showed the least bit of interest in anything about it. I told the driver to circle back around and head to the airport. It was pretty quiet for the ride back. We pulled up to the curb at the airport and I told them to get back home the best way they could. After all, they were in their 30s and 40s and owned twin towers in Houston. Too damn rich to appreciate a damn thing I did for them. The next week, I listed the 1,000-acre ranch for sale in the *Wall Street Journal*."

I guess children who grow up with money and privilege miss the gifts that are given, even the really big ones. The disappointment showed on his face and I could not comprehend such disrespect and disregard for all his money and efforts to leave his entitled children an amazing oasis of beauty.

I walked back to my desk and prepared a folder of documents that he would need to take with him for reference while he was out of the office. With his briefcase in hand, he walked out of his office and up to my desk. "It's time for me to go, Mrs. Marsh. Let me know if I can help you in any way. I'm only a phone call away."

With a smile, I replied, "I will. Have a safe trip."

He walked to Mr. Jordan's office to say his goodbyes and while in his office, the grey-haired cranky lady, Marge, came into my office and shut the door. The serious look on her face let me know that she was not there to ask to be my lunch buddy. She leaned forward and said, "Mrs. Marsh, aren't you the least bit curious about the lady that periodically calls Mr. McCormick?"

I shrugged and said, "Well, no, I guess it could be anyone."

She leaned in a little closer and said with righteous disgust in her voice, "I'll tell you who she is, she's his whore! She meets him up there two weeks before the Mrs. gets there, and he stays two weeks after the Mrs. comes back. Doesn't that make you sick?"

I was in disbelief! My view of the powerful and good man I had looked up to with such respect, now seemed less a man of character than I had once thought. Remembering his seriousness and the question he had asked me about secrets, took on a whole new meaning of the secrets he was carrying and the mysterious double life he was living. After that, I kept my head down and my door shut, doing the work I was hired to do.

A few days after Mr. McCormick had left for the summer, Marge came into my office and shut the door. Her demeanor was quite different this time. As she sat down, she said she wanted to apologize. Her anger towards me stemmed from having worked there for over five years and only being paid $900 per month. "I have been here longer than any other employee," she said. "Imagine how I felt when I found out your salary. I'm not saying I could do your job, but I could have been trained to do the bookkeeping to at least give me a raise."

Marge was starting to cry, so I offered her a tissue from the box on my desk. All I could tell her was that I had no idea how her salary compared to anyone there. We sat quietly for a few minutes, neither of us knowing what to say. I felt the need to explain how I ended up with such a wonderful position and paycheck. "Marge, I gave up two jobs for this position. I have tons of experience with bookkeeping, payroll, oil and gas, and various other work experience. You could take night classes and get a bookkeeping job anywhere for more money than that."

All I could do was encourage her to keep looking for the next best step and not to quit her job until she found it. The tension between us felt less angry after our little chat, I understood what had been behind her coldness towards me and I think she appreciated my encouragement.

Mr. McCormick was very generous to let my family and me have full use of his owner's box at the new racetrack in town. On several occasions, I had taken my husband, sister, and brother-in-law and once I took a whole group of my friends for the afternoon. We were treated to prime seats overlooking the track. There was a full buffet of food and drinks, and we were living large. We made lots of fun memories! My sister especially loved it. She told me the way she picked her winning horse was by how the horse switched his tail on the way to the gate. I thought that was a funny way to pick a winner, but it seemed to work pretty well for her.

The boss was gone for four months this time, staying on the Canadian island he owned. He owned a seaplane that allowed him to island hop or go to a good fishing spot when his sons visited. I now knew there were some other activities that kept him in Canada as well.

The day he returned from this long stay, he bounced in the office with quite a pep in his step. He said, "Come in and sit down, Mrs. Marsh, I've got some good news to share. One of my horses won first place in a race. Yes, *my* horse. I took a lot of pictures and I brought one for you." He was overcome with laughter and could hardly compose himself. He handed me an 8x10 framed photo of his horse wearing a blanket of red roses. He was wearing a white suit with a bright red ascot and stood next to the horse, his wife and the trainer. "I'll tell you, Mrs. Marsh, it's the most fun a man can have with his pants on."

After a few minutes of his excitement, he settled into his big chair behind the desk and said, "I hope it went well with you these past few months. I think you have a good grip on the books and the process for the yacht."

I sat down in the chair across from his desk, "I think it went well, the yacht was brought into dock, they got the barnacles off," I said with a grin. "It's been cleaned and redecorated, and a new lease signed for the next cruise."

"Mrs. Marsh, did I tell you about when I bought the yacht? I planned a month-long maiden voyage to the Caribbean for just my wife and me. We had a five-man crew and all the sunshine we could stand for a month. Every now and then we would go into port to enjoy some sights. One morning while we were docked, I heard a loud noise in the next slip. I looked out the window and there was the most massive yacht pulling right into the slip next to me. That burned my ass! I called the captain and ordered him to pull up the anchors and get the hell out of there. He asked, "Where to?" and I said, 'Out in the middle of the sea, we're not parking next to this big bastard. Let him have it!'"

I was silent, I didn't really understand his anger at the larger yacht. I guess it's an ego thing. I'm not really sure if he ever took another cruise on the yacht after that.

EIGHT

"When one door of happiness closes, another opens, but often we look so long at the closed door that we do not see the one which has been opened for us."
—Helen Keller

Mr. McCormick and his family had returned to Canada, so the office was pretty quiet. One day, I left the office at the end of a somewhat mundane day and crossed the street to the parking garage. Before I entered the garage, I ran into an old friend I had not seen for quite some time. Excited to see me, he told me about a new job he had just landed and wondered if I would be interested in being his assistant. He grinned and said, "I'll pay you more than you are making now." His abruptness startled me and I had to pause and catch my breath before I asked, "Where?"

"It's an insurance company on the third floor of the building you work in now."

I told him I was happy for him, but it was not likely he could afford to give me a raise from my current salary. I had it pretty good where I was with regards to pay. We exchanged pleasantries and went our separate ways.

The following day, I got a phone call from him and he was determined to top my current salary and tempt me away from my current position. I was taken aback by his persistence, but my gut was telling me this was something I should at least consider. After all, the glamour of yachts and a private Canadian island no longer challenged my abilities. I now saw behind the curtain to the reality of what most could not see from the outside: a dysfunctional marriage, ungrateful children, and a certain sadness that money could not fix. I had enjoyed my time there and was lucky enough to have had some great privileges, but God had laid the next step in front of me and like the many times before, it was time to step forward to see where it would lead me.

The insurance industry was not something I knew much about beyond the policies I had bought for Alden and me years ago. It was like stepping into the dark and having to find my way, but I had certainly done that before and felt I could do it again. My new boss, Mr. Rob Holloway, told me to think of this new profession like being on a train. We were the engine that pulled the cars, namely the sales team. He had seven salesmen, all men, of course. Most of the time they were out in the field selling policies, but on Mondays, they would all pile into the office for the weekly sales meeting to discuss the sales they had made and the goals for the new week. It was my job to type up and mail out all the policies that had been written. There were no standard forms stored on a computer to be filled in. These were the days of good ole White-out when you made a mistake. Keeping up with seven salesmen bringing in new policies each week kept my typewriter keys moving fast. Mr. Holloway pushed his team and if they were not meeting their goals there was hell to pay.

As I fell into the routine of the work, the weeks seemed to pass quickly. I made some great friends and learned a whole new industry, but I knew this was just a layover along my journey and I would not linger here long. It had been a nice sidestep, but it would soon be time to move on again. It would be difficult to say goodbye to Mr. Holloway and the dear friends I had made there. I had made some great memories, but I know the job was nothing more than an overpaid typist and insurance was not my calling.

In the days before online everything, the newspaper was the source for job openings. One morning, as I scanned the ads, my eyes stopped on the big bold print that read: NEED EXPERIENCED OIL & GAS PROFESSIONAL. My interest was sparked, and I immediately picked up the phone and called the number in the ad. After a brief but fruitful conversation, I snagged an interview for the next day.

The building was not located downtown where I had become accustomed to working for the past several years. Instead, it was east where there were lots of shops, restaurants, and the big college in town.

The beautifully landscaped building was three stories and all glass with a big atrium in the middle. My interview was not with the company president, but with the secretary. She explained it was a startup and they were looking for someone who knew the business and could hit the ground running. After the seven years I spent with Mr. Roth, as well as the time with Mr. McCormick, I knew more than most who might apply for the position of Oil & Gas Land Executive. I was hired on the spot and asked to start work right away. The position was a definite step up from the insurance company where I felt my skills were not being utilized.

The next day, I broke the sudden change to my boss at the insurance agency. Although he was disappointed, I think he understood it was time for me to move on.

That first morning I showed up for work, I was escorted to the largest, nicest office I had ever been assigned. It was on the ground floor with lots of windows. Everything was first class. There was a uniformed attendant, pushing a food cart down the hallway. She stopped at each door to ask if the person inside if he or she would like anything from the array of breakfast food and drinks on the cart. She came by again at midafternoon. There was a freezer stocked with all kinds of frozen dinners in case anyone decided to work through lunch, which was easy to do with the intense workload of a startup company. These were some of the best job perks I'd had so far. They were certainly a step up from the Styrofoam cup of coffee I had to pay for and ride up the elevator with so many years ago.

My first assignment was to keep track of and be responsible for every single tract of land leased in and around San Antonio for possible drilling production in the area. The term for this exploration is "wildcatting"—going into an area where previously there were no producing wells and drilling to see what might be there—in other words, it was a "wild card."

My boss, Mr. Clive Larson, had somehow secured a two-year contract with some German investors that were pouring money into the company with hopes of a huge payoff. The beautiful office space and all the daily perks led me to believe they must have written some pretty big checks. The posse of landmen in the office were buying up leases at a fast pace and I suddenly found my desk stacked high with land lease agreements for me to keep track of and manage. It was a giant project and I knew why they didn't have time for someone to learn this job. I jumped in with both feet and the days and weeks flew. Before I knew it, it was Christmastime.

Mr. Larson was very health conscious. In fact, he rode his bicycle to work each day. It amused me that here we were in a lavish office atmosphere and the boss would come each morning peddling through the lobby and straight to his office each morning like a guy from a bicycle delivery service. For Christmas, the employees were each given a large basket of mixed fruit. I guess he wanted us to be healthy too.

Mr. Larson was in his late fifties and very physically fit. He was warm and friendly. One special day he drove his car to work and took me and several of the other ladies in the office to lunch. As we drove through a neighborhood on the way to the restaurant, he slowed down next to a house that looked like it was undergoing a remodeling job. He rolled down the window and yelled, "Hi, honey" as he blew a kiss to a middle-aged blonde woman up on the roof. We soon learned that was his wife. She had a full construction crew and spent her time remodeling homes. Throughout lunch I could not stop thinking of her up on that roof slinging a hammer. I grew up in the country, but there were some jobs I just didn't imagine a woman doing, especially the wife of an oil and gas executive.

Our new team of wildcatting trailblazers were getting to know each other and forming friendships. There was a younger gal, Carolyn, who sat near my office and we soon became good friends. She laughed easily and stayed busy at her typewriter. Occasionally, she would make a mistake and yell, "Oh, turkey turds." I couldn't help but laugh out loud and ask, "What did you say?" Disgusted, she'd jerk the paper out of the typewriter and reply, "I messed up, now I have to start all over."

One afternoon, I received a call from a lady, Janice, who worked in the building on another floor. She sounded friendly and said that she had heard that I knew how to crochet and was hoping I could teach her. We made a plan to meet in the next day in the office supply room during lunch. Janice and I met the next day. She was beautiful, bubbly, and bursting with personality. She told me she wanted to learn to make an afghan and since I had made five of them already, I was happy to help. I wrote step-by-step instructions of how to do rows and patterns for her to have when we weren't together. Janice was a quick learner. We continued to meet regularly in the supply room, eating lunch and as Janice called it, "crocheting." It was my little break in the day from the stacks of papers and disappointing news of another dry well. Although we were working at top speed and test wells were being drilled, we had not had a well hit—yet.

I was often visited by a geophysicist who worked in our office. His name was Ed, and he dropped in to say hello when he got up to stretch his legs. He was a small man, bald, and on the nerdy side, but always had a smile on his face and often enjoyed a pecan twirl sweet roll. To say Ed was frugal was an understatement. He kept a box of the small but delicious delicacies in his desk drawer. He never offered anyone one of his treasured treats, never! I soon learned that he rationed himself one pecan twirl per day, so I imagine sharing would have thrown off his allocation for the week. Secretly, Carolyn and I would laugh about his daily twirl, and once, when the office had a break-in, we laughingly decided it must have been the pecan twirls they were looking for. I am certain it was the first thing Ed checked when he arrived at work. I later learned that he did not even share his pecan twirls with his wife.

Each day as I entered work, I would observe the atrium flourishing with beautiful flowers, the birds in the trees, and the goldfish in the pond. From my window, I saw the caretakers busily maintaining the beautiful landscape. Time was passing quickly. The two-year contract from the German investors was drawing near and still not one well had hit anything but dry dirt. I knew this could not go on. I was certain that Mr. Larson had promised the investors a big payout, but I could not imagine what he had told them to have invested the amount it would have taken to sustain this place and all our salaries for two years. I kept quiet, but I knew the outlook was not good since we had not discovered a single producing well.

Mr. Larson called a companywide meeting. There was an oversized bottle of champagne in the middle of the table, rumored to have cost $2,000. He popped the cork and made sure we all had a glass as we waited for the news from the investors. *Would they put more money in and continue the contract? Or would they pull the plug and end their wildcatting days?* I wondered. The phone call came, and the champagne glasses settled on the tables around the room. I could tell by the deflated look on Mr. Larson's face that the days of the snack cart delivering goodies, laughing about Ed's pecan twirls, and supply room crochet session was about to end. As I waited for the investors to come on the line, all I could think was that poor Mr. Larson would most assuredly be riding that bike into his office for the last time. He would give each of the employees two weeks' paid notice. He was about to lose everything, but at least chose to go out with the best champagne the investors could buy.

Having seen the writing on the wall, or rather in the daily reports on my desk, I had already started scanning the newspaper for my next step. One ad caught my eye. It read, "Needed Now: Oil and Gas Management." That looked like it was right on my timeline. I applied with my updated resume and, as if it was orchestrated by God, by the end of the champagne send off, I received a phone call to come for an interview. Once again, God opened the door and placed the step in front of me when it was needed.

NINE

*"You can go as far as your mind lets you.
What you believe, you can achieve."*
—Mary Kay Ash

The gentleman on the other end of the phone said he was impressed with my background in the oil and gas industry and was looking for someone who could start immediately. We arranged an interview, but I'm not sure there was anyone else being considered. The office was located on the west side of town, the industrial side of the city, and much closer to my home.

When I arrived, I was greeted by Mr. Ronan Eckols, a big, burly man with bright red hair. He seemed to laugh easily and informed me it would be a one-woman office. He offered me a generous salary and told me up front that he knew absolutely nothing about drilling an oil well and he sincerely hoped I knew *everything*. Mr. Eckols explained that the company had recently been bought as an investment by a very prestigious family that owned a major NFL team. This was just one more in their portfolio of companies along with racetracks and thoroughbred ranches up East where they lived.

I was a bit surprised that they would entrust their investment with someone who knew nothing about the business, but he chuckled and said, "Sister, you better know everything or at least someone to confide in to get us through." The investors had thought they hired a manager, but I could see he just knew nothing more than how to bluff his way in and I would be the one managing the day-to-day running of the business.

There were 26 wells and an intrastate pipeline through Louisiana and Texas that were purchased. All files would be transferred to the new office and the boxes had to be unpacked and a filing system set up for me to get a handle on the status of each well production. At least I would have complete control of how things were organized since Mr. Echols had no clue what a drilling report looked like. I soon found out that I would also be negotiating the annual contract for the sale of natural gas to the power company, something I had never done before.

Mr. Eckols seemed very busy and was in and out of the office most days. This worked well for me since he offered no help with the daily tasks. I could set my own pace and handle things without his approval.

One morning, he entered the office with a big grin on that freckled face and announced, "We are in the cattle business."

Having heard no mention of this before and not sure how we ended up in that profession, I looked over my typewriter and said, "Really? How and where are we in the cattle business?"

He replied with a somewhat smug smile, "I ran electric fence around that hundred acres we have leased and bought 50 head of cattle to start with and I am going to do that with all those others in that file cabinet."

Realizing that he thought the leases we had meant we had surface rights, I slid my chair out from behind my desk and stood up to look him in the eye. "Mr. Echols, we do not have any rights to the surface on those leases, only for the mineral rights below the property. You can't run cattle or do anything to the land."

A stern look fell over his face and I could see anger creeping up as he realized his lack of knowledge had impacted him in a big way. "Are you sure about this, Mrs. Marsh?"

"Oh, Mr. Echols, I am very sure about this!"

He cleared his throat and as he headed to the door he said, "I guess I better get the fence taken down and the cattle back to the auction barn. Let's don't talk about this to anyone." He didn't return to the office for a couple days and I did not ask about the cattle. My days were so busy I didn't miss my absentee boss, who only occasionally dropped by at his convenience.

In the same office building next door was a small oil well servicing company. The only other woman I saw from time to time in the hallway was a petite middle-aged lady named Dee. We had met in passing and she seemed very serious and soft-spoken. One afternoon, she entered my office and sat in the chair near my desk. All I knew about her was that she kept the books for the service company and rarely ventured out of her office so this visit was out of the ordinary.

She asked if we were the only ones in the office and said she wanted to talk about something privately. She leaned forward and softly said, "Do you know about the hunting trip your boss is planning to Jakarta? He told my boss it was a big oil deal and if he would pay for a private charter plane to take a dozen passengers, he would give him a well to work over when they returned. Mrs. Marsh, my boss doesn't have that kind of money and I don't know how he will afford to do that." This came as news to me and I told her I would start listening and see what I could find out. Since our wells were in Louisiana and Texas, I didn't know what a trip to a foreign country could possibly have to do with this new plan of his.

Two days later, my boss appeared in the office again with a stack of papers that he laid on my desk. He said, "I need your help with these forms to get my passport. What religion are we?" I looked up at his face with a puzzled expression and said, "I'm Methodist." He put his pen on the paper and said, "How do you spell that?"

He started to explain that he was planning on taking some very *important* people to Jakarta to hunt wild game and discuss an oil deal.

I said, "An oil deal—in Jakarta?"

"Yes, yes, it's a shipping deal."

My mind was spinning as I thought of his lack of knowledge about anything to do with oil and gas. I knew he probably knew just as much about shipping as he did about the cattle business. I kept my mouth shut and went back to my work.

The trip lasted five days and when he returned, he carried in a large leather bag that he sat prominently in the middle of his desk. He leaned back in his big chair, smiled, and told me to come look in the bag.

As I unzipped the bag, my eyes were fixed on the stacks and stacks of cash.

He said, "I beat the hell out of them in poker. I left them with empty pockets." He was laughing and proud of himself.

Suddenly, I knew the true reason for the trip, and it had little to do with oil.

Mr. Eckols was a champion marksman and had held the title for several years. There was even a framed cover of a big game hunting magazine with his photo on it hanging in his office. This trip had had everything to do with his love for hunting big game in the wild—and across the poker table. He had scored on both and even talked someone else into paying for the chartered plane.

Later that afternoon, a gentleman in a suit came in carrying a briefcase filled with diamonds, watches, and other jewelry. Mr. Eckols needed a way to hide his winnings that would not show up in the bank. I focused my attention on the mountain of work that waited for me and we did not discuss his trip or his winnings again.

Weeks later, I was informed that the owners of the company would be coming in to visit. I had not been told much about them except that they were a family of great wealth and influence. Mr. Eckols wanted to plan a big catered barbeque on one of their well sites. He said it was one he was having worked over, meaning to pull the pipes, steam clean them, and replace them in the well to increase production.

Guests at the big event would include the bank president, as well as the owners, Mr. Art Sr. and his four sons, and myself. As the only woman in the group, my only job was to sit there and watch the show. Mr. Eckols entertained them with his marksmanship skills. He asked me to choose heads or tails as he flipped a quarter in the air and shot a hole in the side of the coin I chose. He did this over and over again and never missed. He impressed everyone and I suppose that was the point. The big metal pipes were hanging from the top of the rig and the sound of the motor on the derrick muffled out most of the conversations. But as they left, each family member handed him a check for $20,000 to cover the cost of the well servicing they had just seen. No sooner had the big car pulled away from the well site, than the rig men were ordered to stop the machines and return the pipe to the hole. The family would not know of the staged show they had just witnessed.

Over time, I had learned a bit more about the family of owners that I had briefly met at the big rig show. They indeed were a family of influence and wealth. Their main focus was most often on the NFL team they owned, the Pittsburgh Steelers. Bradshaw was a force to be reckoned with and there were few teams that could outplay them.

The end of the year was approaching and the big gas contract with the city would be coming up soon. I asked Mr. Eckols if he wanted me to schedule a meeting for us to go together. He said, "Oh no, I'll be returning to my family home in Wyoming so it will be yours to do. If you are afraid to handle it, then hire someone to do it."

I researched the old records in preparation and learned that there had been no increase in the past four years. After careful calculations, I decided to raise the cost by 1% and this seemed to be a win-win on both sides. This was a new feather in my cap, I could now add city utilities contract negotiations to my wheelhouse.

A few months into the new year while pouring over the drilling reports, the phone rang and the voice on the other end was Mr. Art Sr. He told me that they would be moving me to a new office and to please begin boxing up the files immediately. His voice was calm, and he assured me there was nothing to stress over but that he needed me to do this that very evening.

The following morning when I arrived for work, I was greeted by a female police officer sitting in my office. Mr. Eckols appeared in the doorway and said, "You and I need to go to the post office together."

We walked out to his car and drove in silence several blocks to the post office. I waited in the car while he strolled causally into the post office to retrieve the mail. He handed me the stack of envelopes to hold. Then he reached across my knees to open the glove compartment and pulled out a pistol. He pointed the pistol in the air, looked down the barrel, and said, "I just wanted to show you my new pistol. It's pretty, isn't it?"

I looked him in the eye and said, "Yes, it looks very expensive."

As he continued to closely admire his new weapon, he said, "So, what's happened at the office?"

I shrugged my shoulders and said, "I received a call last night from the owners and they informed me the movers would be here to move the office. I don't know where and I didn't know anyone would be here this morning."

We sat in silence for what seemed to be uncomfortably long. He took a deep breath, leaned across my lap, put the gun back in the compartment, and said, "I just wanted you to see my gun." He turned to the steering wheel and drove back to the office.

When we stepped out of the car, he was greeted by three plainclothes detectives. I walked towards the office building and one of them followed close behind me. We stopped at the door and he leaned in to say, "Ma'am, I followed you to the post office and I kept my eye on you the whole time. You really kept your cool."

It hadn't occurred to me to be frightened until now.

The female officer walked towards me as I entered the office and informed me that the movers would soon be there for me to follow to the new office location. Fortunately, Mr. Art had rented an office space that was convenient to the airport for his future visits and very close to my home. A few hours later, I followed the moving truck with all our furniture and files headed for the new office. I never saw Mr. Eckols again.

Little did I know at the time, but I was headed into five glorious years. The Steelers were on a winning streak, their horse tracks and dog racing tracks were drawing large crowds. The high-profile family seemed to turn everything they touched into gold. They were gracious and giving to me and my family. I had earned their trust and was handsomely rewarded. Soon my husband and I were attending football games whenever they played in a neighboring state. We were flown to and from Dallas and Houston and always had excellent seats. Louisiana Downs racetrack had opened in Shreveport and, of course, they had box seats, which they allowed my family to use and enjoy. We were treated to so many fringe benefits—I felt so rewarded for my work.

Watching the horseraces with my sister and her husband from the prestigious seats at the track, I remembered something Mr. Art had said. He told me that his dad told him and his siblings to never place a bet on a horse race. I thought this fact rather ironic since they owned many horses and racetracks. But he assured me no one in their very large Catholic family had ever bet on a race.

Over the next five years I managed the company on my own and only hired a secretary to type the many reports I had been used to keeping up with on a daily basis. There was a field crew that reported in and payroll to handle for them. The first year was a whirlwind of growth and changes. The owners purchased heavy equipment to use in the oil field and formed an equipment company. We drilled a new well that brought in new excitement and rising expectations for the company. The door seemed to be swinging all the time with visitors and new activity. Four more wells were acquired for the company to operate and manage. I was given a company car to use at my discretion. It was like a dream come true, and for a woman to be in this position was indeed a new era.

Things were moving along pretty smoothly when Mr. Evans, the owner of the two newly acquired wells we now managed, came to visit the office. His private plane had landed at the airport just down the street and he said he had four hours to spare and wanted to check out the operations. Mr. Evans was a very handsome, polished professional from New York. His friendly demeanor made it easy to engage in conversation as we drank a cup of coffee at my desk. He insisted that I continue with my tasks and said he would enjoy getting to see the daily efforts it took to handle the office business. This made me a little nervous, but with all that was waiting on me, my focus quickly shifted. Lord knows, I didn't have time to sit and while away the morning.

The phone rang and it was the field foreman. The Caterpillar dozer needed to be hauled into the shop for repair for the second time in two weeks. The heavy equipment division of the company was set up with the intent of saving money by using our own equipment rather than contracting it out. This was not proving to be going in that direction since the last repair bill was over $3,000. I needed to figure this out so it was not a continual expense. I told the foreman to get the repairs done and please let me know when it was ready. I planned to follow the delivery trailer out to the site to see the situation firsthand. I hung up the phone and turned my attention back to the stack of files on my desk. Mr. Evans looked over a report he was reading and said, "Mrs. Marsh, you could not work for my organization. I own many companies and I can tell you that you that you must learn to delegate your work to others."

I refrained from the response in my head and politely smiled and said, "Thank you, Mr. Evans. I will remember that advice." *Just who did he think I was going to delegate all this to?* I wondered. I was a one-woman army except for the typist and the field crew who had already managed to ring up several large repair bills. I could see Mr. Evans was used to having plenty of people to handle the issues that arose, but I didn't have that luxury. If you want to see that things are done right, some days you have to put on your boots and follow the trailer out to handle it yourself.

The next call that came in was from the attorney. He called with instructions for me to prepare an umbrella policy and then set up a meeting with the insurance company. In the meantime, the postman walked in with a bundle of mail to sort through, which I happily "delegated" to Shelia, my assistant. After a few hours of reading through reports and other information, Mr. Evans came to my desk and announced his driver was here to take him back to the airport. We shook hands and he said, "It was very nice meeting you. I know my wells are in good hands and I hope we can talk again before Christmas."

I walked him to the door and told him it was my pleasure to meet him and that I looked forward to speaking with him soon. I was glad to get back to work without the audience but felt I had made a good impression.

Three days later, the dozer had been repaired and they were ready to deliver it to the site. I had dressed in slacks and carried a pair of boots in the car as I followed the big trailer carrying the dozier down the bumpy backroads where they were digging the intrastate pipeline. The crew had been working on pulling pipe through a wide area of a creek. Once the dozer was unloaded, I watched them begin their usual plan to use the dozer to drive across the boggy divide and drag the pipe through the mud and the muck. As I sat there watching, big clumps of mud piled up on the freshly repaired dozer. I yelled to the foreman, "STOP!"

I asked the foreman, Redd, what he did to get all the debris out of the pipe when he got it across the other side. I could clearly see what was causing the need for so many repairs to the dozer as it sat deep in a trench of fresh mud.

"Oh, Mrs. Marsh, we will blow some air down the pipe and clean it out when we are done" he said.

"Please send someone to the pipe yard and bring back a cap for the end of the pipe and have your men walk across the creek and carry it across," I said.

A little surprised that I had just out-calculated two of the issues that caused their problems, he sent a man to the yard to bring back a pipe cap that would fit the end of the pipe.

"Now drive the dozer across the bridge to the other side and pull the closed pipe across from where the men put it," I instructed.

The foreman and his crew were not used to taking orders from a woman on such matters, but went about carrying out my plan. I felt as if I had solved two of their problems: the dozer would not need to be hauled in every couple weeks to clean out the engine, and time would be saved not having to blow out the pipeline after it was pulled through the trenches. I'm pretty sure there were some timid looks on their faces as I kicked off my boots and headed to the car. It wasn't every day they took orders from a woman.

By the following July, the office was running smoothly enough for me to take a 10-day vacation with my family. Shelia could handle the daily reports and pay the bills until I returned. My family had patiently waited to shift gears and enjoy some new scenery and this was the perfect opportunity. We planned a trip to Washington, D.C. with my sister and brother-in-law. Alden and Melanie were excited and counted the days until we departed. My brother-in-law's sister and her husband lived there. He was the U.S. Ambassador to France. They showed us all the historic sites, the capital, JFK's grave, and the Washington Monument. This was a long way from that small country town near the Louisiana border. It gave my mind time to rest and enjoy new adventures. At the end of the 10 days, I was glad to get home and took a little time to rest before returning to work.

The following week at the office, I received a call from Mr. Art. He told me that in a few days, a of couple men would be coming to the office to look over the records and make an evaluation on the company. He assured me my job was safe and that they were just trying to get the value of the company and its assets.

The day they arrived at the office, I spent hours answering their questions and digging out all the latest reports. It was a big task, but I could tell they had done this before. At the end of the week, Mr. Art called me again to assure me they were not selling the company and my job was safe. This made me breathe a little easier until late that fall when it happened again.

This time it was a different group of men. They spoke broken English, but I had no idea where they were from. They just mumbled among themselves and got straight to work. Again, I got a call from Mr. Art telling me they were not selling the company, it was just to get an evaluation for the records. I truly hoped this to be true. After five and a half years, I truly loved this family and all the freedoms and benefits they had blessed me with. Leaving them would be difficult, but as these incidents had made me somewhat nervous, I once again began to watch the Sunday newspaper's job ads.

There it was right at the top of the page, a large bold ad that read: NEED NEW MANAGEMENT FOR LARGE OIL COMPANY IN DOWNTOWN SHREVEPORT. On a half-cocked notion, I sent in my resume to see what would happen. Three days later, a phone call came from the personnel manager of the company. The interview was conducted over the phone and I was blown away at the six-figure salary that was offered. My hard-earned college degree was paying off in a big way. I was hired over the phone and asked to start work on Monday.

This was a lot to take in and I wasn't sure how would I break this to Mr. Art and his sweet family. With all the auditors still in the office and Shelia handling more of the daily tasks, I decided to hold off with this big news, at least for a few days, until I could figure out a smooth transition. Things could run as they were for a few days.

My first day on the new job I was told that one of the company planes was fueled up and ready to take me to San Angelo, Texas. There was a business meeting they needed me to attend on their behalf. This felt like jumping into the unknown, but I had managed that before. I began to eat the peanuts they had provided and drink the Coca-Cola, hoping it would get rid of the huge lump in my throat. I had not had the opportunity to even visit the new office or give notice to Mr. Art. Just before takeoff my brick-sized cell phone rang from my purse. It was Mr. Art.

"Mrs. Marsh, what's going on?" he asked.

I took a deep breath and said, "Mr. Art, I have accepted a phenomenal job offer. The kind of offer, if I was your sister you would tell me to jump on."

He paused and said, "How much?"

"It's a solid six-figure position at a very large prestigious company downtown."

He responded with a surprised, "Good Lord, you do have to take that! You have earned that position and I am very happy for you. Don't worry, with how smooth things have been working and with Shelia taking on more responsibilities, we will figure out how to handle things for your transition to the new company. You do feel like family and I do not want to lose touch."

As I ended the call with Mr. Art, I couldn't help but hold back some tears. What an incredible journey it had been, all the happy memories of the NFL games we had attended, touring his thoroughbred ranch, the trust and confidence he had put in me. He had provided a giant step forward for me to solely manage his business, but it was time for me to step forward in what was ahead.

My mind settled as I looked out the window as we approached the runway in San Angelo. There were no tall trees, only wire fences and scrubby bushes. West Texas was indeed a different world.

A car and driver met me at the airport to take me to the office. As I rode past the unfamiliar buildings along the way, I noticed a very large building. The building looked brand new, but the grounds were grown up and it looked vacant. There were weeds in the walkway and the enormous building sat dark and lifeless. Finally, I arrived at the office and was greeted by a young blonde lady. She softly shook my hand and asked if we could speak privately before I met with the executives.

She was careful to look around as we stepped into a small office just off the hall. She explained that a group of employees had appointed her to ask me a question they hoped to get answered from the corporate office. Leaning in and lowering her voice, she said, "Why are all the employees getting let go after three months only to be replaced by someone new? We have seen this time and time again regardless of their job performance."

Having no real understanding of any of the situation I had just walked into, I told her I would relay the message and see what I could find out. She seemed slightly satisfied and thanked me for keeping the anxiousness of the employees from their boss.

We stepped out into the hallway and she led me to the boss's office and then quietly walked away.

TEN

I am a strong woman. Everything that's hit me in life I've dealt with on my own. I've cried myself to sleep. Picked myself back up and wiped my own tears. I have grown from things meant to break me. I get stronger by the day and I have God to thank for that.
—(Anonymous)

I sensed I was stepping into a situation that would require me to navigate with caution, at least until I knew more of the background.

I walked into the office, greeted the senior administrator with a handshake, and sat down in the chair across from his desk. Once the formalities were out of the way, I asked about the enormous vacant building. He smirked and told me it was supposed to be a new hospital but that someone had made a big goof. The day it was completed, as soon as they started to move the hospital beds into the rooms, they discovered that every doorway was too narrow. "You can just imagine the lawsuit that ensued," he said," and it has sat empty ever since. I am sure someone lost their shirt on it and I would hate to be that guy."

Having that mystery solved, I turned my attention back to the reason for my visit and asked to see the field inventory. He pulled out a file from the stack on his desk and I began to look it over and compare with a list I had been given in advance. Conversation turned to silence as I sifted through pages and pages that were placed in front of me. My observation of the discrepancies and the new knowledge of the rotating employees were adding up to the main reason I had been sent by the home office. There were numerous inconsistencies and suspicious irregularities that made it clear there was a fox in the henhouse and I was looking right at him. It was now almost 2:30 in the afternoon and I closed the last file in front of me. Unsure if he was aware of my deductions, I thanked him and called for the driver to take me back to the airport.

As I buckled my seatbelt aboard the private plane, the pilot announced we needed to hold our position for another plane to land on our runway. Little did I know, the next plane to land was the other company jet. It brought in five male executives to escort the senior administrator from the building and then change the locks on the doors. I later learned that while sending me on a fact-finding mission, they had been doing their own discovery of bank records and contracts. Maybe I was just a distraction to keep him occupied while they plotted their strategy to surprise him. I had been a witness once again to the mischief and deceptions of this business. My previous employers had prepared my awareness to the lies and secrets that seemed to be a part of the good ole boys club.

I returned to my new office high above the city sidewalks.

In the coming weeks and months, I was tasked with obtaining four new state leases in Jackson, Mississippi. It was quite the feather in my cap to be one of only two female landmen (no feminine form available for this term) in the tri-state area. The other female soon became my close friend, Martha. We shared many a conversation about the boys' club and the elite Petroleum Club that was exclusively male. Having a first name that suggested I was male, I actually received an invitation to join, but when they found out I was a female, the invitation quickly became null and void.

My experience grew with the vast holdings and interest the company held. They even owned a coal mine and processing plant in Kentucky. There was plenty of reading to do with each new thick file put in front of me. Anyone with as little as $5,000 could become an investor, so this made the correspondence with each shareholder quite a big task.

For such a large company, the filing system was a mush pot of confusion. In fact, there didn't seem to be any system at all. They had a big beautiful library of books and information connected to an oversized room of file cabinets and even a full-time librarian to assist employees looking for information. But as the files got thicker and the investors grew in number, whatever system they had must have been thrown out the window. Trying to locate information on anything in there could turn into a search and rescue mission. I knew there had to be a better way.

I began working with Kay, the bubbly lady who worked in the library. She was detail-oriented and would make sure that everyone abided by the system we put in place to keep things in order. I think the oil business was new to her and the many walls of cabinets had been overwhelming to her since she didn't understand how the information was connected. When she began to grasp an understanding of the wells and the documents connected to each one, we put together an color-coded system to help make the maze of information less confusing. There was even a separate storage room for all the geological maps that were necessary to understand the leases and units the wells were categorized by. Over the days and weeks of working together, Kay and I chatted. It was not hard to hear office gossip in a company so large.

We occupied four floors of the tall downtown building, so there was always some whispering going on around coffee pots and bathroom doors. Although I never went looking for the updates on office happenings, the young gentleman in the next office felt it was his responsibility to keep me informed. He had talked extensively about my first day experience of how that senior administrator had doctored the books and what had already been suspected before my visit there. I wish I had that insight before I made the trip, but I didn't have Ryan, my inside information source, then. Ryan proceeded to ask me if I knew about the scandalous stories that had been steaming up breakrooms all over the executive floor. When I said no, he lowered his voice and told me that four married men from the executive group had taken a business trip to Florida with four of the very young office assistants. When they returned, all four girls were sporting diamond earrings, necklaces, and bracelets. His eyebrows raised as he smirked and said, "And we all know what they did to get them. I can walk you through the office right now and show you their bling; they love to show it off."

I laughed and said, "No, thank you Ryan, I will take your word for it," and got back to work.

As the weeks turned into months, I was surrounded by young eager landmen who were new to the company, some new to the industry altogether. Having worked longer than most of them had been out of diapers, I became a resource for answers to their questions. Most were single and just out of college, not many years older than my Melanie who had just graduated from high school. Regularly, they would attend a special lunch at the Petroleum Club and stroll back in the office with the smell of cocktails on their breath, laughing about some tall tale my boss had told them. My boss was most likely one of those four men who went on that Florida trip.

Ted was my direct boss and I thought it best not to be involved in the speculation and opinions that made up the whirlwinds of office politics. Ted was a rather short, cocky man who walked with an air of authority over the department. He was older and married, but he had an eye for the young ladies and was often seen patting them on the derriere. Frequently, those looking for promotions would be found sitting in his lap while he heaped on the compliments in hopes of whatever they were willing to accommodate.

He was not the only one in the boys' club who kept the large glass windows steamed up. The chief financial officer, Mr. Snowden, would often stop by the office manager's desk, to look over her shoulder, and probably her low-cut blouses, to read the newspaper she was holding. Many days there was whispering from behind the paper, as she batted her eyes and giggled at his flirtations. They were both married and seemed to be closer than most coworkers should appear. They had been caught kissing behind more than one doorway after coincidently ending up in the breakroom or supply closet at the same time. I kept my head down and chose to be no part of the conversations about the outwardly inappropriate meetings in her office.

I had not met the owner and CEE of the company, Mr. Landry—a high roller who had taken the company he started to a publicly traded company in only a few short years. He lived large and spent large. The offices were decked out with custom carpeting and lighting throughout the executive floor. It looked more like a hotel lobby than a place of business. Beautiful paintings hung in prominent focal points. Mr. Landry's office, which I caught a glimpse of when I visited Eloise, his secretary, had a custom rug with a large oil derrick in the middle. It was quite a sight to see and was rumored to have cost some major bucks. All the executives were men, of course, with luxury company cars and fat expense accounts, as well as a full-paid membership to that elusive Petroleum Club.

Mr. Landry liked doing things his way and was not accustomed to needing approval from 13 board members as was required after the company was taken public. He still owned a majority of the stock, but the power struggle between his way of doing things and the board became too much for him. One evening after what had been an explosive board meeting, Mr. Landry had his expensive rug rolled up and all his personal files packed only to reopen another office directly down the street. He kept his interest in the company and started over without the disagreements of the board members. His Vice President, Mr. Ted Oxenburg, stepped in as acting president. He was a short man with a big attitude and hot temper. His expensive suits and flashy gold jewelry confirmed he was a man who liked the finery as much as Mr. Landry. He used explicit language and carried himself with an air of arrogance similar to Napoleon.

A few days passed after the changing of the guard and Ryan was back at it signaling me to his office for his latest update. The aspiring young girls in the office were giggling and sitting in Ted's lap during lunch the day before and Ryan couldn't wait to share the details. Having pretended I listened with any amount of interest, I told him I need to make some phone calls before noon. Just before leaving his office, Ryan also told me that everyone would be getting an end-of-the-year raise in our next paycheck. This put some spring in my step. I was already happy with my salary, but a raise sure would not hurt.

The next day when the paychecks were passed out, Ryan popped his head and my doorway and said, "How did you like your raise?"

Not having opened the envelope on top of my stack, I grabbed it and ripped it open. As I pulled out my check, I looked up at him and said, "My check is exactly the same, there is no raise."

Ryan said, "You need to talk to Ted. I was told everyone would get one."

I rolled my chair back and assumed it was a payroll mistake. I got up and headed for Ted's office. He motioned me in as he was finishing a phone call.

"Ted, I didn't get the pay increase in my check that the others received," I told him.

As he pushed the tall-backed chair away from his desk, he gave a look of condescension and said, "Mrs. Marsh, you make a lot of money—for a woman."

I felt an instant fire welling up inside, *For a woman?* It was as if my gender directly limited my ability to be smart enough or earn as much as any of the young guys in the office who had been running to my door for reassurance on leases they had never seen. I stood there and in the deafening silence gave him a glare that I was sure would ignite his hair on fire. In one smooth turn on my heel, I walked to my office, picked up my phone, and called Mr. Landry's new office. Though I had never met him personally, I knew Eloise, so when she answered the phone, I asked if Mr. Landry would be needing any help with his new company. I explained the situation and after she relayed the message, I could hear Mr. Landry in the background say, "Tell her to come immediately. I have a raise for her and she can get our land department up and running."

That was all I needed. I grabbed my purse and my personal belongings and walked out the door down the three blocks to his office. I left ole Ted to figure out just what he lost and what I was really worth.

My feet couldn't carry me fast enough as I walked with new determination. Eloise greeted me with a big smile and said, "We are so happy you are here." She showed me to my new office that had few furnishings other than a desk and a chair. It was the true sign of my new beginning.

Mr. Landry had not wasted one minute putting together his new company. This time there were no board members to please. He had a knack for rolling the dice big and making money. His drive and ambition were never lacking for the next big deal. I had the land department up and running in record time and the employee list was growing by the week. Shortly after I began work, Mr. Snowden, the financial manager, came over to join the team. I imagined that his friend the office manager was disappointed to see him leave and would have a lot more time for her job without all the secret meetings. However, since they were only a short walk away their secret meetings continued.

Within the first year we again occupied most of the office space on three of the floors in the office building he leased. His beautiful rug with the custom oil derrick anchored the elaborate décor of his office. The expensive wood furniture he sat behind as he made the big deals had been delivered from the interior decorator who was hired from California.

The California decorators also put in a new private dining room for the employees with a chef who prepared delicious meals. The dining room and the rest of the office were elaborately decorated with inlaid stone floors, grasscloth wallpapers, and tropical palm trees placed around the corners of the room. Expensive pieces of artwork were strategically placed for dramatic effect. No expense was spared on the furnishings and décor of the offices. My office was no exception; it was beautifully furnished with a stunning wood desk and credenza, artwork, and lamps.

As the deals got bigger, several land men had been added to the department and each one was awarded a luxury company car since a good deal of their time was spent out in the field acquiring lease agreements. Though I did not get a company car, I always traveled in style on the company plane when a trip was required.

Mr. Landry asked me to travel to Mississippi in hopes of winning the bid on some state-owned mineral rights. He said that the four corners of the state of Mississippi were coming up for a blind bid process to award the mineral rights to the highest bidder. I would have only one shot at it, or so I was told.

Upon arriving at the Jackson airport, I rented a car

and found my way to the office in Meridian, where I was to meet with the state officials. I entered the room and shook hands with the four well-dressed businessmen who were already seated. They were spaced around the round table and each had a big notepad in front of them. As the meeting began and the bid process was explained, I noticed each of them started writing something on their notepads. Trying not to be distracted, I glanced at the tablets in front of them and noticed they were all doodling and drawing pictures on their notepads. Not taking notes, not writing words at all, but doodling! As the conversation continued, I wondered if their doodling was some sort of secret code or just random scribbles on the page. After all, the bids were submitted blindly and the state could ultimately award the bid to anyone they wanted. Of all the meetings I had been a part of over the years, I had never seen a group of men doodle and draw as if they were kindergarteners. The meeting ended and I patiently waited with the others in the lobby to see if I would be returning with the leases. My suspicions told me the bid would be awarded to whoever they liked best and not some blind bid. Fortunately, they must have liked me best because I waked out of there securing the state-owned leases for the company. *Maybe I should take up doodling,* I thought.

In the midst of all the land department business, my office door was kept busy with all my notary work and not only for the company. Word had gotten around the building, so other oil and gas businesses and companies were soon coming to me to do all their notary work—a lot of notary work—and payment for each piece of it! At first, I kept it quiet, but as the files got thicker and the outside visitors were growing in number, I knew I had to tell Mr. Landry. *No need to put my good job in jeopardy,* I thought.

"Mr. Landry, I must be the only notary in this big building because everyone seems to be bringing me things to notarize and I don't want it to interfere with my job. How do you feel about this?"

He smiled, leaned forward, and said, "Mrs. Marsh, you do all you want to do, you know I believe in making money when you can." This was such a relief to me since it was becoming a daily event and I was now earning as much for my side notary gigs as some made from a regular paycheck. I started keeping a log and billing the outside companies each month for the notary work. What a blessing!

As the four-year mark approached, the oil and gas market saw a drop in prices. Production in the Carolinas had increased to such volume that there was a surplus and no one was buying. With all the various ventures, Mr. Landry, and most companies, had overextended themselves, putting everything at risk just to survive. Changes would have to be made and cost cuts everywhere. First to go were the expensive company cars the executives had become accustomed to. There were angry executives storming in and out of Mr. Landry's office. Many tossed the keys at him and quit. Those who had been his friends and allies when the money was rolling in and times were good now turned against him and showed no empathy for the difficulties he was facing. The elaborate dining room was closed, and the chef let go. Even with all the cost-cutting, it was not enough to change the outcome. In the coming months, all the employees were let go, attorneys were coming after Mr. Landry and even his own attorneys were trying to collect payment. Everything had been leveraged but the bleeding of money could not be stopped.

Mr. Landry called me into his office and closed the door. He told me that he would be closing the office and moving to a small office down the street but that he could not afford to take a single employee with him. As he sat there with a somber look on his face, he said, "Mrs. Marsh, I have lost my home, my cars, and even the jewelry off my body. I had one of my own attorneys corner me in the parking lot and take my Rolex watch and wedding ring as payment."

In that moment, all I could feel was sadness for his loss. I knew I would be fine, but he had lost everything he worked for. He had ridden the wave to the top and been knocked down before, but this time he was older and had lost more than ever.

It was only a short time later that I found my next opportunity with one of the few oil companies that had managed to not go under with the oil crash. I knew I would be okay as God had guided my steps so many times before. A few months passed, and not having a way to get in touch with Mr. Landry, I sent word through a mutual friend that he was in a small office downtown and hoped that I would come see him for some notary work he needed to complete.

The next day I planned for a two-hour lunch break so we would have plenty of time to handle what was needed. I stopped to pick up lunch on the way to his office and decided to bring some extra sandwiches since we would be meeting through my lunch hour. As I entered the old rundown building, I could not help but notice the stark contrast between the beautiful offices he had left behind to wind up here. I stepped onto the rickety old elevator and pushed the button for the third floor. The lighting was dim, and the smell was musty as the sound of my heels on the old wooden floor echoed down the empty halls. I am not certain, but he may have been the only occupant on the floor. I knocked, opened the door, and saw Mr. Landry and his wife working side-by-side behind a small metal table, much different that the extravagant wood desk I had seen him behind so often. Mrs. Landry sat quietly as she typed on an old typewriter.

Mr. Landry asked me if I had some stamps for some outgoing mail he hoped to send out. I smiled and started digging in my purse to hand him the book of stamps I had recently purchased. I sat the paper bag of sandwiches and drinks on the table and I could see the gratitude in his eyes as he pushed his papers to the side. I noticed the empty space on his wrist and ring finger and remembered how he had told me the attorney took the Rolex watch and ring from him in order to collect on the debt he owed. Feeling his embarrassment as he noticed my glance, he cleared his throat and said, "Mrs. Marsh, thank you so much for coming today, I appreciate your belief in me and your friendship more than you know."

I notarized the stack of pages in front of me and refused any payment. My conscience would not allow it. With the last page complete, all three of us left the office together and walked towards the elevator. I could see his ambition to build his empire back was still there, but his body was weak, and his youth was gone, and the likelihood was small. As we rode down in the rickety elevator, there was a sudden jolt as we hit the bottom floor which caused Mrs. Landry to drop part of the load she was carrying in her arms. The half sandwich I had tossed in the trash can fell out of her bag. She moved quickly to wrap it tighter in the cellophane paper and said, "Oh, I was taking that for our supper." My heart was heavy knowing that what was left over from our lunch would now be their dinner that night. We paused briefly as I hugged them goodbye and returned to work.

For months, Mr. Landry believed that he could turn things around and regain what he had lost. I was always happy to help when he called with a request. The stress was wearing on his health and the frailties of his age were showing. It wasn't long before I received a phone call letting me know he was in the hospital and asking for me to come notarize papers his attorney had prepared. I entered the room to see Mr. Landry withered and frail sitting in a wheelchair. I suspected the purpose was to put his things in order. My heart was heavy as I knew I had witnessed the rise to extravagance and the loss of it all. Failing had never defined him; he believed he could get it all back, but he just ran out of time. Two weeks later I was notified that he passed away. Once again, I was witness to the reality that wealth and status is something you can't take with you into death.

"I shall pass through this world but once. Any good therefore that I can do or any kindness that I can show to any human being, let me do it now. Let me not defer or neglect it, for I shall not pass this way again."
—Henry Drummond.

My journey has come full circle, ending in a similar place as where it all began, saying goodbye to a boss, a mentor and a friend. Someone who believed in me and gave me opportunities few women in my day had. It is a rich journey of experiences, lessons, and friendships laced with secrets and trust.

As a young working wife and mother, I entered each new doorway of opportunity with hope, excitement, and a determined spirt. Each opening molded me into a seasoned professional. Although I faced fear and uncertainty along the way, I learned I was stronger than I knew and was as well-equipped as most of the men I worked alongside. The decades of rich experiences and the relationships along the way are the things I continue to carry with me.

Now in my eighties, as I reflect on the twists and turns of the years and the wealthy, affluent people I have worked with, there is a common thread: All lived a life of grandeur, but most were lonely behind the façade of a luxurious lifestyle. Even so, they all had lessons to teach and stories to tell. I share their stories with purpose and gratitude for the journey—for the threads of each life have spun a fantastic intertwined carpet that carried me from place to place. As with most journeys, each incremental landing was part of the ultimate destination. Where we go is marked by beautiful landmarks of friendships along the way. Time does not pass; it continues without us, taking with it only the stories and parts of ourselves we shared.

LESSONS I LEARNED FROM HELEN

These are just a few of the many memories I have of how she impacted the lives of others and inspired me throughout the many highs and lows in life. Her light still shines bright long after she is gone:

See the opportunity to help someone help themselves

It was normal for Helen to arrive at her office at the NASA lab very early. She managed a group of workers who assembled intricate parts under a microscope that went into galvanometers. One morning, she was at her desk, looking out the window as she answered phone calls from some of her co-workers who were making excuses for missing work that day. As she hung up the phone, she noticed an old car parked in the parking lot and saw a young Asian woman sitting alone inside the car. Helen's compassion and concern prompted her to leave her office, walk across the parking lot, and approach the young woman.

It was somewhat hard for them to understand each other because of the language barrier, but Helen's invitation to the young woman to come to her office was finally received.

Once inside, the young woman was able to tell Helen that her husband worked in the factory across the parking lot, but they could not afford rent until he received his first paycheck. The only food they had was a case of peaches, which they ate every day in the car.

As Helen listened, she noticed the woman's small, delicate hands. She gave her a tour of the operation, showing her what was needed. She offered her a job starting at $15 an hour. That was a lot of money in the 1960s. The woman was not only very appreciative, she was a quick learner. She worked there for over five years without missing a day of work, and Helen often said that hiring her was one of her best decisions.

She and her husband moved when his job was transferred. On the day of her departure, there were hugs, and tears of appreciation, all because Helen had looked out the window, saw someone in need, and extended an opportunity.

Something that seems small to you can make a big difference to someone else

I remember when Helen took our family on a 10-day vacation to Monterrey, Mexico. Helen, my husband Alden and I, and our parents joined her. We traveled in style in her new air-conditioned Cadillac—complete with a hired chauffeur. In the 1950s, this was a true luxury vacation for our Hill Country family. At the end of our stay in Mexico, as we headed back through the dusty barren desert back to the States, Helen said, "Before we reach the border. I want to make a stop. We can save some time and do a good deed all at the same time."

We pulled off the road and headed to a small rickety shelter. As we got closer, we saw it was more like sheets of old tin propped up in the trees. Several children stood in the shade of the trees near the shelter. Alden and my sister got out of the car and walked through the heat and the dust towards the children. As they got closer, a petite Mexican mother stepped toward them. Helen reached her hands out, opened her palms, and offered her all our Mexican currency. The woman took it in her hand and then gave Helen a big hug. The mother began to cry as they walked away.

As the two of them got back into the car, Helen said, "We didn't change their lives, but at least we made it a little more comfortable."

There is power in numbers even when buying toilet paper

As a special treat to her employees, Helen chartered a bus to take them for a day trip to a casino just over the Mexican border. She enjoyed arranging fun activities for her hard-working employees. They had a good time at the casino—some won and some lost, but what made it most memorable was what happened on the bus ride back.

Helen asked the bus driver to stop at a small rundown store on the side of the highway. It looked almost abandoned and you could tell they had not seen many customers in quite some time. She stood up and asked all 40 of the passengers on the bus to please go in the store and buy something—it didn't matter what—just something. Everyone got off the bus, including the driver. He discovered a popcorn machine just inside the door, asked for a large kitchen bag, and began popping the corn. With all 40 passengers crammed into the two small aisles of the store, they bought the shelves almost bare. The driver had purchased the bag filled with popcorn and 40 plastic cups to share with the passengers.

Helen was the last to get back on the bus. She then asked everyone to trade and share items with each other, so they could all have a variety of items from their shopping trip. Laughter erupted as they all began trading items from their purchases. As the bus reached their destination, one man who had bought a sack filled with toilet paper now had one roll left and a bag of assorted items. Most of all, what they all left with were great memories and a new understanding that there is power in numbers. If each person just does a little, the impact can be big, and what you take home is more than you expected.

Helen was my mentor, a keeper of secrets, an encourager, and an entertainer. She could make me laugh and show me how the simplest of things make a difference in others' lives.

AFTERWORD
by
Melanie Townsend

*"Every experience God gives us,
every person He puts in our lives,
is the perfect preparation for
the future that only He can see."*
—Corrie Ten Boom

WHEN MY MOTHER firmly requested that I her help share the stories and secrets she had kept for so many years, I was slightly annoyed at the thought of the task she insisted I take on. I thought of many reasons why I was too busy or not the right person for the job. I found out I was the perfect person for the job. It was such a gift and a blessing to be able to step into my mother's shoes as a young career woman and mother, to see through her eyes as I never had before.

I recognize the courageous steps it took for a young girl from a small farming community to step into the next challenge that was put in front of her. With an upswept high hairdo and wearing Jackie Kennedy fashion, she always stepped forward with unbridled courage and rose to any occasion even when, as was often the case, she was the only woman in the room. My awareness became magnified as I came to understand all the sacrifices and determination it took for not only my mother but for so many mothers and women before me who paved the way. The movement of woman empowerment began long ago with women in all industries taking steps of bold courage we may never know. The doors that were opened for myself, my daughter, and those who follow should never be diminished or forgotten. We are surrounded by women with intriguing stories and accomplishments who came before us if we only take the time to listen to their stories before they are lost.

Those who walked before us illuminate the path we now walk upon. May we all widen it for those who follow after us.

11-18-20

Judy,
 we have a lifetime connection.
Love you forever.
 This is my true footprint
of many years of jobs. Let
me hear from you.

        Luv u

          Maurice Marsh

Judy,
Hope you enjoy
the book!
    Love,
     Melanie

Made in the USA
Columbia, SC
13 November 2020